ENDO

Our ability to grow in the Assemblies of God will depend in large part on our sustainability of younger generations. *Called* not only provides the heart behind this enormous task in identifying young people in our churches who feel a call to ministry, but it lays out a clear and intentional path for young people to be mentored, discipled, and prepared for a lifetime of ministry. *Called* is a phenomenal resource for every pastor or leader who works with young people. It will be a gift to the body of Christ for generations to come.

MELISSA J. ALFARO
Executive Presbyter Representing Under 40 Ministers
Assemblies of God

Called is a must read for everyone who hears the voice of God calling them to step out in faith and say yes to their divinely designed adventure in ministry leadership. John Zick gives a powerful framework for approaching the call to full-time vocational ministry. By providing practical principles to pursue the call, John answers the questions that young leaders should be asking.

KENT J. INGLE
President
Southeastern University

I'm grateful to John Zick for creating a go-to book for pastors and young leaders who desire to follow Christ in full-time ministry. The information in this book will be a guide with practical steps and compelling insights to be successful in ministry.

SAM RIJFKOGEL
Lead Pastor
Grand Rapids First Church

In 1985 there were 1.4 billion unreached people globally. Today there are over 2.4 billion in 7,000 distinct people groups. The need is greater now for young men and women to be called into full-time missions than ever before.

This book will help you add competencies to your calling and prepare you for a lifetime of serving Jesus for His glory among the nations – whether you are called to go or called to send.

DICK BROGDEN
Cofounder of the Live Dead Movement
Saudi Arabia

Often in our ministries, the pathway from the altar to the pulpit for a student is blurry. *Called* by John Zick is a clear and concise guide for students who sense the call to go into ministry. This book will inspire them, challenge them, and most importantly encourage them. It's a must read for all who are sensing the call of God on their life for vocational ministry.

PETER REEVES
NextGen Pastor
Mount Hope Church

As crazy as it may sound, I first felt "called" to ministry in a drama class my sophomore year of high school. Mr. Davis asked the class to write down what we saw ourselves doing ten years from that day. I sensed God speaking to me in that moment and I wrote, "Youth pastor in Honduras." My calling would be confirmed many times over the next several years.

I wish I'd had access to an incredible tool like John has created. *Called* provides a framework for developing both as a follower of Jesus and as a developing leader. I highly recommend this book to you.

JEFFERY PORTMANN
National Director
Church Multiplication Network USA

CALLED

Cover the Earth with the Love of Jesus

JOHN ZICK

GPH®
Gospel Publishing House

02-4280

ISBN: 978-1-60731-646-6

23 22 21 • 1 2 3

Printed in the United States of America

CONTENTS

FOREWORD

Every student who has felt a call to ministry needs this book in their hand as soon as possible. Contrary to popular belief, you don't have to wait until you graduate high school, earn a college degree, or get your first "real job" to start pursuing the call God has on your life. A person's lifelong journey to fulfill their destiny really happens one day at a time, one step at a time. *Called* challenges you to start taking those steps now! Through personal stories, biblical support, and practical teaching, John will help you understand how to start walking in your calling. I believe we will see an increase of qualified pastors, missionaries, church planters, leaders, and more because of this resource.

Doug Clay
General Superintendent
The General Council of the Assemblies of God

INTRODUCTION
DEFINING MOMENTS

If you've spent any amount of time growing up in church, you know a salvation call in children's church typically means the same kids come to the front repeatedly – sometimes every week if a salvation call is offered. Even if they've already accepted Christ months (or years!) before, they respond to the altar call every time to ensure that they are, in fact, saved. Or maybe they don't fully grasp what "being saved" means.

I can relate. The first ten thousand times I responded to the salvation call in children's church, I was afraid of going to hell. But one day after I prayed, I felt different. Even as a seven-year-old, I clearly remember feeling excited to give my heart to Jesus. I couldn't wait to tell my parents that I had accepted Jesus into my heart – again. But I think they knew this time was different too. We prayed together, wrote the date in my Bible, and from that moment on I felt the call of ministry on my life. **Even though I didn't audibly hear God's booming voice from heaven or experience a dove landing on my shoulder, I had a peace about it—I just knew I was called.** It was what I like to call a "defining moment" in my journey.

However young or old you are, if you are reading this book, it's most likely because you have experienced a defining moment in your life as well – you have been called to ministry!

Let me clarify: As believers, we are all called to ministry. Jesus commanded all believers, "Go into all the world and preach the Good News to everyone."[1] We all play a part in God's plan to ***cover the earth*** with the love of Jesus. A common proverb heard today is, **"I can do things you cannot, you can do things I cannot; together we can do great things."**

God has created each of us with a unique and distinct purpose, meaning we all have a responsibility to share the gospel. Fortunately, we're not all called to accomplish that in the same way. Some will do great things as teachers, janitors, architects, doctors, politicians, bus drivers, road workers – the list goes on and on. The point is: We all have a specific purpose and make up the perfect body of Christ. We'll discuss it more in a later chapter, but the body of Christ is the universal Church and consists of all believers worldwide.

First Corinthians 12 describes this principle and the importance of it further:

> **The human body has many parts, but the many parts make up one whole body. So it is with the body of Christ. Some of us are Jews, some are Gentiles, some are slaves, and some are free. But we have all been baptized into one body by one Spirit, and we all share the same Spirit.**
>
> **Yes, the body has many different parts, not just one part. If the foot says, "I am not a part of the body**

because I am not a hand," that does not make it any less a part of the body. And if the ear says, "I am not part of the body because I am not an eye," would that make it any less a part of the body? If the whole body were an eye, how would you hear? Or if your whole body were an ear, how would you smell anything?

But our bodies have many parts, and God has put each part just where he wants it. How strange a body would be if it had only one part! Yes, there are many parts, but only one body. The eye can never say to the hand, "I don't need you." The head can't say to the feet, "I don't need you."

In fact, some parts of the body that seem weakest and least important are actually the most necessary. And the parts we regard as less honorable are those we clothe with the greatest care. So we carefully protect those parts that should not be seen, while the more honorable parts do not require this special care. So God has put the body together such that extra honor and care are given to those parts that have less dignity. This makes for harmony among the members, so that all the members care for each other. If one part suffers, all the parts suffer with it, and if one part is honored, all the parts are glad.

All of you together are Christ's body, and each of you is a part of it.[2]

Together as believers, with all our different passions and abilities, we create a perfect masterpiece. Because not one of us is created the same – in looks, passions, thoughts, or experiences – we're not competing against each other. We complement one another in God's design for this world and work best when we work together to accomplish His will.

This book, however, is specifically for those who feel a vocational call to the Church. Maybe you feel called to be a missionary, evangelist, pastor, or church planter. Maybe you aren't sure yet.

The important thing is that you know God has chosen you to carry out a particular part of His plan. First, that is amazing! Congratulations! Second, this is the perfect book for you. It's been written to help you prepare for and navigate the next steps of your "called" journey.

After that moment in my living room, my passion and the desire to pursue the call God placed on my life never left, even when my relationship with Jesus and my personal calling both were challenged and questioned.

It was a little easier during my years in junior high when it was "cool" to be a Christian, which was rare (especially for a public school). I'd regularly stand in the lunchroom announcing at the top of my lungs that my youth group was doing an outreach or hosting some event. I would hand out trendy invitations as my classmates walked out the door, and I would do it all proudly!

Then as high school hit and the coolness of being a Christian ended, I realized that living for Jesus was no longer contributing to my popularity. As I began to feel the tension of keeping my friends or choosing Jesus, I faced another defining moment in the process of seeking my calling.

During my sophomore year, I was home one Friday night because I had turned down another invitation to a big party. I was filtering through the questions I asked myself many times throughout high school: *Why am I doing this? Why shouldn't I just go to the party? Does anyone even notice? Am I really making a difference?*

Moments later, my Motorola razr flip phone buzzed, interrupting my classic Snake game (did those details just date this story?). My best friend was texting to say I still had time to get to the party. I thought, *I'm just going to do it. One party won't make a difference*. But as I walked out the door, I felt the voice of the Holy Spirit say, "You have to choose: Do you want to be popular and keep your friends, or do you want to live for Me?"

I knew this defining moment was more than just a one-time decision whether to go to a party or not. I was choosing the direction I'd go in my teenage years and all the years to follow. I came back into the house, shut the door, and texted my friend that I wasn't coming. That was the very last text I received about weekend parties.

I'd love to tell you the rest of my journey was simple and easy, and that was the only hard decision I had to make before I entered into ministry. But, it was simply setting the stage for many more moments of intentionally choosing Jesus.

If you feel like you are called to ministry, but you're only pursuing it so that one day you can be famous, make a lot of money, wear cool clothes, and speak in front of millions of people, *this is not for you*. Those things may come – and they do for some people. But you have to be willing to obey God's call even if you know you may be the least in every situation, you may be overlooked and underappreciated, and in twenty years, you may finally be financially stable enough to pay off your college debt. But, if you can feel totally fulfilled despite those things because you're exactly where Jesus wants you, then this will be the job for you!

Obviously, some of the things listed are extremes. A mentor of mine always said, "Pray for the best, but prepare for the worst." No cookie-cutter approach to ministry exists; everyone's journey will look different. The point is: Don't accept a call to ministry for personal fame or glory. Make sure your motives are pure, you have a genuine heart for God's people, and you are being obedient to what God is calling you to, not anyone else.

This leads to why I wrote this book. As I looked at my own life and the lives of others who have walked and are walking this journey, overcoming challenges and experiencing defining moments, I saw a pattern.

Each chapter of this book is dedicated to one of six principles that I found to be a common thread through the journeys of people who pursue their ministry calling. Here is a brief overview of what you will learn about these specific principles:

Build Disciplines – The habits you create and establish now will last a lifetime. Be intentional about how you spend your time and choose carefully what you allow in your life. These principles don't come naturally or easily – they're intentionally built over time with the goal of growing and grounding you. Start by thinking of these three areas: **spiritual health** (your closeness with Jesus), **mental health** (your awareness of yourself), and **relational health** (your closeness with others). And as you do, remember that with self-discipline, you can do almost anything.

Start Serving – The core of any ministry position is servanthood. Don't wait for a four-year degree or years of ministry experience – just start where you are and with what you have. One major mistake many people make is waiting until they feel qualified or until they're asked. So, take initiative and find areas to serve the people around you! Consider the various ways to serve in your **home**, ways to serve in your **church**, and ways to serve in your **community**. If you learn what servanthood means and practice it now, you'll save time and a knock on your ego in the future.

Seek Community – Look for people in your life who will help **develop**, **encourage**, and **stretch** you. Don't wait for people to seek you out – seek them out! We all need a strong spiritual mentor in our life, so start by finding your Paul (develop). Paul was a spiritual father to many believers and took time to invest in Timothy's life. Then, find your Barnabas (encourage). Barnabas was an encourager and friend who could be counted on. This is the type of friend everyone needs to do life with. And finally, find your Timothy (stretch). He received a life-changing investment from Paul. Especially in ministry, we can lead and invest in others, like Paul did for Timothy.

Discover Gifts – Our creative God has uniquely designed every person to fulfill a specific part of His plan. He has placed various abilities, passions, and talents in you – tools He wants you to use to fulfill the calling on your life! You were created with these gifts in you, but like any skill they must first be discovered, then developed properly. We'll be highlighting these five spiritual gifts: **apostle, prophet, evangelist, pastor,** and **teacher**.

Learn Passions – What is your "holy discontent"? Holy discontent is feeling uneasy about the brokenness in the world and taking action to change or fix it. So, what issue in the world can't you stand? What problem do you want to see solved? What has God placed within you to change? For Moses, it was that the Israelites were mistreated slaves. For Martin Luther King, Jr., it was the unfair treatment and oppression of people of color. Start thinking about why God put you on this earth and why He has called you to ministry. Three things you can start with now are: **Be self-aware, don't compare,** and **guard your heart**.

Never Arrive – There will always be areas in your life that you can grow in and ways to keep learning and becoming. You should never feel as if you have arrived; that's a dangerous place to be! It's healthy to remember that you are a part of the big picture, but you are not the big picture itself. Four ways to ensure you keep growing in a healthy way throughout your journey include: **Ask questions, learn from anyone, don't believe the hype,** and **seek different voices.**

These six principles aren't a guarantee for success, but as we dive deeper into each, you will begin to see a road map for healthy ministry. Living in the calling God has for your life is the most rewarding and valuable thing you can do on this earth. But you have to be intentional about walking this journey. It won't come easily, and it won't happen accidentally. Being called to ministry is a full-time job and requires a genuine heart, a sacrificial attitude, and a desire to ***cover the earth*** with the gospel and lead people closer to Jesus!

So, before we get started, take some time to inspect your heart. Be honest with yourself and with others about your motivations. Dig deep and ask the Holy Spirit to open your eyes to where your perspective, opinions, thoughts, and beliefs may be self-focused instead of God-focused. Then open your ears to hear how He wants to remedy that.

When you're ready to start, remember not to rush through this book.

- Sit on a chapter for a while. Have your Bible and a journal with you to process and reflect on what you learn.
- Ask the Holy Spirit to reveal specific things to you. Test the content against the Word of God.
- Ask for clarity and insight from spiritual counselors in your life.

This book is short enough that you can read a chapter a few times and choose one or two things you want to work on before moving to the next chapter. Now, find a good reading nook, grab your favorite beverage, and get ready for the journey!

Notes

1 Mark 16:15.

2 1 Corinthians 12:12–27.

CHAPTER ONE
BUILD DISCIPLINES

In high school, I read a devotional about praying without ceasing.[1] *Well, that seems impractical,* I thought. *How can I pray all the time?* With sports, school, friends, and everything else important to a sixteen-year-old, I didn't know how I could do all of those things while also praying nonstop. Can you imagine? "Sorry I missed the catch, Coach. My eyes were closed because I was praying!"

As time passed, I couldn't stop thinking about it. I had to figure out what it actually meant. I finally went to my youth pastor and asked how it was possible to pray constantly with everything I had going on. He explained it like this: Praying without ceasing is an *attitude*. It's a practice of making Jesus a part of our daily lives, not just sitting with our heads bowed and eyes closed all day long. And we're urged to pray without ceasing because God wants to have a relationship with us! No prayer is too big or too small for God; He simply wants to be involved in our lives. We invite Him to be involved when we talk to Him.

No prayer is too big or too small for God; He simply wants to be involved in our lives. We invite Him to be involved when we talk to Him.

We see this idea play out in the Parable of the Persistent Widow, an illustration Jesus used to encourage His disciples to never stop praying.[2] Simply put, a widow continually visited an unjust judge, asking him to give her justice against her enemy. Her request was so persistent that the judge helped her because he couldn't take her visits any longer. The point is, if an unjust judge hears our request, how much more is our loving Heavenly Father ready to hear us and act on our behalf when we call out to Him?

I'm not going to tell you that building this spiritual discipline was easy because it wasn't. Even after choosing to make Jesus a part of my daily life, many times I would be getting ready for bed and realize it was the first time I was praying that day – sometimes it was the first time I was even *thinking* about Jesus! But I would excuse it and tell myself, *No big deal. I'll do better tomorrow*. The cycle continued day after day, week after week. **No matter how hard I tried to build this discipline, I couldn't seem to get into a pattern of praying without ceasing.**

Then one night it hit me: *I can ask Jesus to help me make Him a part of my everyday life, right?* It might sound kind of sad, having to ask for help to make the Savior of the world a part of my day. But in reality, there is no shame in asking for help when you're having a hard time, or you know you can't do something on your own. After that prayer, I got the idea to put reminders in my phone so that every hour it would buzz with a prompt to pray.

It was a process. There's this idea that it takes 21 days to build a habit. But according to a 2009 study, building a new habit can take anywhere from 18 to 254 days – the average being 66 days.[3] Looking back, I recognize that it took several months of my phone buzzing, stopping everything I was doing, and saying a quick, simple prayer before I noticed a change.

At some point, I realized I was actually *beating* the reminder buzz. I was including this mindset, this attitude of praying without ceasing into my daily life – and it was becoming a habit! I was growing and the spiritual disciplines I was asking God for were becoming real.

Obviously, building this discipline was not easy. **Even if you are determined to build a specific discipline in your life like I was, it doesn't mean that it will come naturally or without some sort of effort on your part.** It takes intentionality, it takes diligence, and it takes time. But, the investment you make when establishing disciplines always pays off and the results are totally worth it!

One of the most famous men in the Bible, Paul was a leader and teacher in the Early Church. In the thirteen New Testament books he wrote, Paul covered various topics including spiritual disciplines. He spoke from experience, because he had one of the most miraculous transformations in all of Scripture.[4] His conversion on the road to Damascus was a call to advance the gospel, which meant he had to shift from persecuting Christians to recruiting Christians.

Apostle Paul

He had to break *years* of bad habits and replace them with new ones – habits that glorified Christ and brought hope to the people around him.

One of his books, 1 Corinthians, is a letter to the church of Corinth addressing some of the serious problems in the church and providing godly counsel and guidance. At one point, Paul specifically focused on the intentional training that must take place to successfully discipline ourselves spiritually: "So I run with purpose in every step. I am not just shadowboxing. I discipline my body like an athlete, training it to do what it should. Otherwise, I fear that after preaching to others I myself might be disqualified."[5]

"Run with purpose." What does that mean? In Scripture we are told that we – all people – were created *on* purpose *for* a purpose. Beginning in Genesis 1, we read that we are made in God's image,[6] which means every person has tremendous value in God's eyes. He knows everything about us – our passions, thoughts, struggles, triumphs – even before we are formed in our mother's womb because He planned for you and me![7] To honor God and His purposeful creation,

In Scripture we are told that we—all people—were created *on* purpose *for* a purpose.

like Paul, we should run with purpose. It's the least we can do for the Creator of the world, the One who knit each of us together and gives our lives meaning.[8] Again, it will take time and effort on our part, but sacrifices are worth making to build habits and disciplines that will move you forward into your calling.

In his autobiography *Just As I Am*, the great evangelist Billy Graham shared many moments in his own ministry journey when he had to choose to run with purpose. These stories tell how he would practice his preaching any time he could, regardless of the occasion.

During his college years, he was invited to preach over the summer – which for most students is a sacred time to do absolutely nothing. But, Graham seized those opportunities because he saw beyond what was right in front of him. One particular summer, he had an opportunity to participate in a two-week evangelistic series. Graham said, "I was developing the basics of my own preaching style and my approach to giving the invitation to come to Christ."[9]

How did he do this? While staying with Reverend Cecil Underwood, Graham said he would walk the streets around Underwood's house practicing his sermons and praying. This

Rev. Billy Graham

is the reason millions came to know Christ under Graham's ministry – he ran with purpose! Even though he had to sacrifice things like his summer vacation, Graham saw the importance of developing his gifts and establishing habits because God had called him to something bigger. And the intentional investment in building these disciplines sustained him for over sixty years of healthy ministry.

The spiritual disciplines we need to sustain us in life don't come naturally. Think about sports. While natural talent or ability contributes to success, that's only part of the equation; discipline is a basic part of athletics. What can make or break an athlete is the determination to work hard and dedication to their training.

We know the average person can't pick up a tennis racket and serve an ace to Venus or Serena Williams or lace up their spikes and beat Usain Bolt in a sprint. It takes a lot of time and effort – hours, months, and even years of practice – to build endurance or perfect form and technique.

Venus and Serena Williams

This idea isn't just limited to sports. Maybe you want to create music like Ludwig van Beethoven or paint masterpieces like Leonardo da Vinci. Maybe you are passionate about science like Marie Curie or innovative technology like Steve Jobs. These "greats" didn't become great without commitment and hard work. Regardless of what interest you are pursuing or goal you are hoping to achieve, the idea is the same: "Discipline is the bridge between goals and accomplishment."[10]

It's safe to say that the disciplines you create will last a lifetime. So, what behaviors, actions, and practices are you repeating? Whether they lead to good or bad, life-giving or draining, effective or ineffective habits, all depend on what you do on a day-to-day basis. It may not be fun. It may feel tedious. It may be hard to see the long-term effects. But every decision you make and action you take affects what you do in the future.

For example, choosing not to cheat on a test can help train your brain not to steal. Or learning how to navigate a fight with a friend instead of giving up can teach you how to address conflict in your marriage. The list can go on and on. The point is, the choices we make may seem small, but they have lasting effects. This is why we, as believers, have to be deliberate and purposeful about the habits we create. Habits, routines, and disciplines don't come naturally – they are built over time, which means we get a say in what we build.

> **"Discipline is the bridge between goals and accomplishments."**

I had no idea how hourly reminders on my phone would affect many other situations over the course of my life. In that situation I knew my end goal – the habit I wanted to build – was to pray without ceasing. And that little buzz set the tone (no pun intended) for how I was choosing to discipline my body to do what it should. **Success for believers is fulfilling our God-given destiny.** God calls people to professions, communities, and even seasons; but it still takes intentionality and discipline on our part to achieve success in those areas.

If you are reading this right now, it's likely because you feel God calling you to ministry. (Cue inspirational music.) That is what God created you for – it's the purpose He had in mind for you even before you were alive! You are a part of His ultimate plan to ***cover the earth*** with His love. Here's the thing: Your calling is bigger than you are. That statement might sound scary, but the Bible promises that we are not in it alone. The Bible says, "If God is for us, who can ever be against us?"[11]

Fires die when they're not being fed, so what will you do to keep your fire going?

So, hear this as all of the possibilities and opportunities you will have while pursuing your calling. Hear it as an assurance that God will lift you up as you trust in Him and His ability.[12] Hear it as a prompt to ask God to help you "accomplish . . . . good things."[13] Hear it as a guarantee that with God, nothing is impossible.[14]

Pursuing your calling is a lifelong process. At times, you won't feel very excited or inspired to push through – that's normal. Fires die when they're not being fed, so what will you do to keep your fire going?

MAKE IT PLAIN

There are three areas in your life where you can (and should!) start building healthy spiritual disciplines now. You don't have to wait until you graduate high school, get a degree, have a family, or get that dream job. Prayerfully consider how you can start now with what you already have.

Spiritual Health

Your Closeness with God

Your spiritual health should be the top priority in your life. Jesus demonstrated the importance of an intimate relationship with the Father, and what better example to follow than the Son of God?

During His time on earth, Jesus made it a priority to be alone with God; He regularly withdrew from the crowds, His disciples, and the general demands of ministry to spend time with God.[15] There were a number of times when Jesus went away to pray – from choosing His disciples to preparing for His death on the cross.[16] But the reason was the same: Jesus desired to connect with His Father in heaven, to talk to Him and hear from Him, to be sensitive to the Holy Spirit, to gain the wisdom and power that only comes when we spend time alone with God.

Learning to trust and obey God – establishing a relationship with Him through the discipline of prayer –

helps us build a solid foundation. And when our foundation is built on Jesus Christ, the Solid Rock, there is no storm that we won't be able to withstand.

> **"Anyone who listens to my teaching and follows it is wise, like a person who builds a house on solid rock. Though the rain comes in torrents and the floodwaters rise and the winds beat against that house, it won't collapse because it is built on bedrock. But anyone who hears my teaching and doesn't obey it is foolish, like a person who builds a house on sand. When the rains and floods come and the winds beat against that house, it will collapse with a mighty crash."[17]**

Sadly, people sometimes take shortcuts in building their foundation. Maybe they take the easy route, compromising on things that are important to them or settling for how things have always been done. Taking shortcuts is appealing because it can be faster, easier, and seem better; but when the storm hits, it exposes all the ways a person has cut corners.

Taking shortcuts is appealing because it can be faster, easier, and seem better; but when the storm hits, it exposes all the ways a person has cut corners.

This happens to people who are called to ministry. There are too many stories about people in ministry who fail because they weren't disciplined when it came to building their foundation. Even if it was unintentional, they formed bad habits – sacrificing quality for efficiency. It's incredibly important to heed the advice in Matthew 7 by investing time and effort into building a strong foundation the right way. There is a difference between knowing the right thing and training yourself to do the right thing – that is where disciplines come in!

Mental Health

Your Awareness of Yourself

Having the knowledge of who God created you to be is not only powerful information to know, but also crucial. Your true identity in Christ is not about anything external – grades, jobs, finances, or appearance. **It's about *who* you are and *whose* you are.** You need to know, understand, and accept that you were created in the image of God.[18] He has a divine plan and purpose for your life so you can impact others through the ministry He has called you to.

Yet, we have an enemy who has come "to steal and kill and destroy."[19] The devil is not the little cartoon figure on your shoulder debating with the angel on your other shoulder. He is a deceiver, a schemer, and a liar at his core.[20] The last thing he wants is for you to walk in the fullness of who God created you to be.[21] Instead the devil is doing everything in his power to make you believe the lies that you are ill-equipped, unqualified, and incompetent to fulfill your calling.

He may tempt you with comparing yourself to the people around you; he may try to convince you that you

Darby Zick

didn't really hear God's voice; he may guilt you with past mistakes all in an effort to distract you from becoming a healthy person and leader. This is why we need to be aware of who he is and guard against his schemes.

Growing up, my mom said the same thing to my siblings and me *every single day* as we left for school: **"Remember who you are."** It's a simple statement, but those four words have stuck with me and challenged me more times than I can count. Who am I? Who are you? According to Ephesians 1, we are loved and chosen by God; we are adopted into His family; we are redeemed and forgiven; we have the hope of being with God for eternity.[22]

These truths are just that – truths. That means our identity in Christ cannot and will never change based on anything we do. For me, understanding these truths provided a greater sense of my spiritual identity as a child of God and helped me to accept it for myself. You need to live life out of the identity God has designed you. You were created on purpose for a

That means our identity in Christ cannot and will never change based on anything we do.

purpose by the ultimate Creator. The One who spoke the earth into existence breathed His breath into your lungs.[23]

You are not a mistake; the gifts, talents, and passions you possess were intentionally given to you so you can fulfill the call God has on your life. No one else can do what you do like you. **As a part of the body of Christ, you are essential to God's plan for the world.** Living confidently in that knowledge frees you to do what He has specifically created you for.

Relational Health

Your Closeness with Others

When speaking to His disciples, Jesus made a rather bold statement about loving one another: "So now I am giving you a new commandment: Love each other. Just as I have loved you, you should love each other. Your love for one another will prove to the world that you are my disciples."[24]

The Bible tells us that healthy relationships are the most important things in life, the most important being our relationship with God. But here, we're going to focus on our relationships with the people around us.

Take a minute to really hear this: If we can't have healthy relationships with others, the world – those we have been put here to reach – will not be able to tell the difference between a nonbeliever and a believer. That's not okay. We are called to be set apart, not to conform to the behaviors

If we can't have healthy relationships with others, the world—those we have been put here to reach will not be able to tell the difference between a nonbeliever and a believer.

or practices of the world.[25] Our ability to establish and maintain healthy relationships will naturally set us apart from the culture.

The apostle Paul told us that believers are to show compassion, kindness, humility, gentleness, patience, forgiveness, and love to those around us;[26] yet too often there is hurt, misunderstanding, and pride in people's hearts that can cause or contribute to broken relationships. It can be challenging to kill those negative emotions and treat others better than they treat us. It's not our human nature to give people the benefit of the doubt. When we are hurt or taken advantage of, we can feel angry, disappointed, or bitter.

However, we are called to reflect Christ's love to those around us and ***cover the earth*** with it. The qualities listed above are all reflected in Jesus Christ – He was kind, compassionate, patient, loving, and forgiving. As we model these qualities in our relationships, we are actually becoming more like Jesus. And the more we look like Him, the easier it becomes to see people as He sees them – as sons and daughters of God who were created in His image – and treat them like He would.

First Corinthians 13, also known as the "love chapter," gives us more specifics about what Christ's love looks like:

> **Love is patient and kind. Love is not jealous or boastful or proud or rude. It does not demand its own way. It is not irritable, and it keeps no record of being wronged. It does not rejoice about injustice but rejoices whenever the truth wins out. Love never gives up, never loses faith, is always hopeful, and endures through every circumstance.**[27]

This is how Jesus loves us! **We don't get to pick and choose when to apply this information.** If more people would approach every relationship with this verse as their guiding principle, there would not be as many issues in establishing and preserving healthy relationships.

How can you start building health in these three areas now?

Read the Bible. The Bible is the inspired Word of God. It has the power to change us from the inside out, so we need to spend time reading it if we want to grow and establish health in these areas. The Bible gives advice, helps us to make good decisions, encourages us to overcome old habits, and teaches us to have self-control. Most importantly, it helps us learn the truth about Jesus and ourselves. We gain a deeper understanding of God's heart toward us. I like to say it's the ultimate cheat code for life. We can trust what it says, but before we can trust it, we have to know it.

Journal. Write out your thoughts. Journaling offers general health benefits: it can manage stress, boost your mood, and help process thoughts and emotions. It's a great discipline to have! Journaling allows you to write down what God is speaking to you, how He's working in your life, and what you're learning as you walk with Him. One of the best parts about journaling is that you have a written account if you ever need to be reminded of God's promises when circumstances are telling you a different story.

Pray.[28] It can be a hard discipline to learn especially in our fast-paced culture, but simply sitting and spending time with God is essential. No time is ever wasted when it's spent in His presence; the One who intentionally created you wants to be in relationship with you. God has a specific will and design for your life. Spending time in His presence helps you know what that plan is. It's crucial that you invest in your relationship with Him: express your thankfulness, tell Him how much you love Him, and set aside time to sit and listen to Him speaking to you.

Creating and establishing disciplines doesn't happen overnight – it's a process that will take time, effort, determination, and intentionality. Even learning how to build disciplines can take time, so don't hurry through this content. Prayerfully consider the call God has placed on your life and ask Him to help you determine what disciplines to invest in and develop now.

Take some time to answer the following questions and share them with someone you trust.

1. From this chapter, what stuck out to you the most? Why did it stand out?

2. Out of the three areas—spiritual, mental, or relational health—which one do you feel the most disciplined in?

3. Out of the three areas, which one do you feel like God is challenging you to get better in?

4. What are some lies that you have believed about yourself and what truths will you replace them with?

Check out more resources regarding disciplines at:

called.ag.org

Notes

1 1 Thessalonians 5:17 (KJV).
2 Luke 18:1–8.
3 Phillippa Lally, "How Are Habits Formed: Modelling Habit Formation in the Real World," July 16, 2009, accessed January 28, 2021, https://onlinelibrary.wiley.com/doi/abs/10.1002/ejsp.674 (accessed January 28, 2021).
4 Acts 9.
5 1 Corinthians 9:26–27.
6 Genesis 1:27.
7 Psalm 139:16; Jeremiah 1:5.
8 Psalm 139:13–14.
9 Billy Graham, *Just As I Am* (San Francisco: Harper San Francisco, 2007), 58.
10 Jim Rohm as quoted in Justin Bryant, "Discipline Is the Bridge Between Goals and Accomplishment" *SelfMade Success*, May 27, 2016, accessed January 28, 2021, https://selfmadesuccess.com/discipline-is-the-bridge-between-goals-and-accomplishment.
11 Romans 8:31.
12 James 4:10.
13 2 Thessalonians 1:11.
14 Luke 1:37 (ESV).
15 Matthew 14:23; Mark 1:12–13, 35; 6:46; 14:32; Luke 5:16; 6:12.
16 Luke 6:12–13; 22:39–44.
17 Matthew 7:24–27.
18 Genesis 1:27.
19 John 10:10.
20 John 8:44.
21 Ephesians 3:19.
22 Ephesians 1:3–14.
23 Genesis 2:7.
24 John 13:34–35.
25 Romans 12:2.
26 Colossians 3:12–14 (NIV).
27 1 Corinthians 13:4–7.
28 In Matthew 6:5–13, Jesus gave us a clear outline on how to pray.

CHAPTER TWO
START SERVING

Many of us have heard of Anne Frank, a young Jewish girl forced into hiding from the Nazis with seven other people after the Germans invaded the Netherlands. Frank kept a diary during the two years she and her family lived in a secret room. She wrote about what life was like in hiding: bathroom schedules, blackout screens on the windows, studying and writing, her thoughts and feelings. She even penned letters and fairy tales. Frank's writing gives readers an inside look at what her family endured and sacrificed during the German occupation.

Can you imagine living in such a small space with that many people, but never being able to leave? Imagine having people sneak in food just so you could survive another day or not knowing if today would be the day you would be discovered and sent to a concentration camp. Despite the situation she was in, Frank lived with the understanding that no one becomes poor by giving. Do you believe that?

Anne Frank

Some people think this refers only to maetrial goods. Four outside helpers were bringing food, supplies, and news about the war into the Secret Annex. But I think that the deeper meaning behind these words is about serving others through giving our time, energy, resources, and attention.

Serving is about putting the needs or interests of others above our own, and not expecting anything in return. With the right heart and intention, you don't serve to *gain* something from someone; you serve to *give* something to someone. So, let's adjust the wording for our purposes: No one has ever become poor by *serving*.

This idea of service is important for everyone, but even more so for someone called to ministry. Why? It's the last thing Jesus modeled for His followers before He was arrested, put on trial, and killed. The Last Supper is one of several events described in all four Gospels.[2] It was literally the last meal Jesus shared with His disciples, hours before His crucifixion. During this time, He revealed someone would betray Him. He blessed the bread and wine that symbolized His body and blood. However, only the Gospel of John recounts Jesus washing the feet of His disciples.

This idea of service is important for everyone, but even more so for someone called to ministry.

Wait! He washed the feet of His disciples – at the dinner table?

If I knew I were eating my last meal, I would not be thinking about serving the people I was dining with, *especially* if the lesson meant touching their feet! I would be more concerned with how the steak was cooked and whether I got the best seat at the table, making sure my last hours on earth were exactly how I wanted them. But that's not the heart of Jesus. **He wanted to leave a lesson with these men, a statement on servanthood He hoped would be repeated in the future.** But He didn't just tell them; Jesus demonstrated this incredibly challenging and eye-opening lesson.

> **Before the Passover celebration, Jesus knew that his hour had come to leave this world and return to his Father. He had loved his disciples during his ministry on earth, and now he loved them to the very end. It was time for supper, and the devil had already prompted Judas, son of Simon Iscariot, to betray Jesus. Jesus knew that the Father had given him authority over everything and that he had come from God and would return to God. So he got up from the table, took off his robe, wrapped a towel around his waist, and poured water into a basin. Then he began to wash the disciples' feet, drying them with the towel he had around him.**
>
> **When Jesus came to Simon Peter, Peter said to him, "Lord, are you going to wash my feet?"**

Jesus replied, "You don't understand now what I am doing, but someday you will."

"No," Peter protested, "you will never ever wash my feet!"

Jesus replied, "Unless I wash you, you won't belong to me."

Simon Peter exclaimed, "Then wash my hands and head as well, Lord, not just my feet!"

Jesus replied, "A person who has bathed all over does not need to wash, except for the feet, to be entirely clean. And you disciples are clean, but not all of you." For Jesus knew who would betray him. That is what he meant when he said, "Not all of you are clean."

After washing their feet, he put on his robe again and sat down and asked, "Do you understand what I was doing? You call me 'Teacher' and 'Lord,' and you are right, because that's what I am. And since I, your Lord and Teacher, have washed your feet, you ought to wash each other's feet. I have given you an example to follow. Do as I have done to you. I tell you the truth, slaves are not greater than their master. Nor is the messenger more important than the one who sends the message. Now that you know these things, God will bless you for doing them."[3]

In Jesus' day, foot washing was a necessity and an expected part of hospitality. The roads were dusty and filled with animal waste, and people wore sandals which meant their feet could (and would) become very dirty. Usually, the washing was performed by the lowliest servant, which is why it's so surprising that Jesus took the towel and did this task Himself. In this moment, Jesus redefined what leadership means. He showed that it is not about position and authority, but about serving.

In this moment, Jesus redefined what leadership means. He showed that it is not about position and authority, but about serving.

Even before this meal, Jesus shared this idea with the disciples. In Mark 10, when James and John asked to be seated to the right and to the left of Jesus in heaven, He said to them:

> **"You know that the rulers in this world lord it over their people, and officials flaunt their authority over those under them. But among you it will be different. *Whoever wants to be a leader among you must be your servant, and whoever wants to be first among you must be the slave of everyone else.* For even the Son of Man came not to be served but to serve others and to give his life as a ransom for many."[4]**

People are naturally motivated by power, but it's a well-known fact that power can corrupt. According to a brief in the *Psychological Science Agenda* newsletter, "Some leaders may be tempted to use their power in self-serving ways."[5] The brief then lists a number of negative behaviors that can result from gaining power.

Jesus knew this about us. He knew about the pride, vanity, selfishness, and desire for self-glory humans carry in their heart (whether we admit it or not). It's human nature, and not assigned to any one person, group, or time period – people like James and John desired power and position in biblical times, just as you and I do now.

When I was growing up, my dad owned a construction company. I loved going to job sites and walking around as if I owned the place because my dad was the boss, the man in charge, the head honcho. It was even more satisfying when people started recognizing my face – I'd give them a head nod as both a greeting and an urge to get back to work. Oh, how I thought I had arrived! On the drive home after watching my dad in his element, I would ask him about being the boss and listen as he talked about how each person played a part and had their specific role. I would interrupt him, "Sure, but what if they don't listen to you or do what you ask? You could fire them, right?"

He would tell me being the boss wasn't about that. *Not about that? What do you mean?* In my mind at that age, it was all about that! Looking back, I learned a crucial lesson on leadership in

Steve Zick

those moments: **Our lives are not about ruling one another, but about *serving* one another.** My dad modeled that servant-leader mentality to me. He was still the boss, but he had determined in his heart that he wanted to serve those under his leadership rather than expect to be served by them. That's countercultural thinking. But if we are going to ***cover the earth*** with the gospel, we have to be ready to think differently!

What society often tells us is that the leaders who are in their positions have a right to be there. Maybe they put in the work, said the right things, or connected with the right people. And because of their efforts they "deserve" their position. But leadership is a gift from God, not a right. "Leaders who understand that leading others is a privilege understand that leading, first and foremost, is about service."[6] This "Golden Rule" of leadership is exactly what Jesus was trying to teach the disciples – that the higher you move up isn't about gaining more power or authority or influence, but about gaining opportunities to serve. Jesus made it perfectly clear that in the Kingdom, "The greatest among you must be a servant."[7]

"Leaders who understand that leading others is a privilege understand that leading, first and foremost, is about service."

That's what Jesus was demonstrating in washing the feet of His friends. If the Savior of the world was willing to humble Himself to the job of the lowliest servant, how much more should we seek opportunities to serve the people around us? With James and John, Jesus saw the condition of their hearts and took the time to address this mindset and correct it. **He said, "Among you it will be different," meaning that we, as believers, should follow His example in putting the needs and interests of others above our own.**

And when we don't follow His example, allowing arrogance and the desire for power to motivate us, we will reap serious consequences. For example, Ezekiel 28 tells us that the devil held a high-ranking position in heaven. He possessed power and influence among the angels, as well as great beauty and wisdom.[8] However, pride filled and corrupted his heart. Instead of worshipping God, he wanted to be worshipped!

Did you know that? It wasn't until the devil decided that he wanted the glory seat that he was judged and cast out of heaven:

> **"How you are fallen from heaven, O shining star, son of the morning! You have been thrown down to the earth, you who destroyed the nations of the world. For you said to yourself, 'I will ascend to heaven and set my throne above God's stars. I will preside on the mountain of the gods far away in the north. I will climb to the highest heavens and be like the Most High.' "[9]**

It's wild to think this self-serving attitude has been an ongoing temptation since the beginning of time. And it likely will never go away; our natural tendency is to say *I*, *me*, and *my*. "*I* want to be honored," "Serve *me*," "*I* want to hold the power." But Jesus said the opposite. He challenges our sinful, selfish nature and tells us to serve and honor others. He tells us to empower the people around us.

He challenges our sinful, selfish nature and tells us to serve and honor others.

This ***cover the earth*** mentality is a part of kingdom culture: using your gifts to serve one another,[10] humbling yourself and thinking of others' needs before your own,[11] finding freedom in Christ and serving others in love through that freedom,[12] and choosing to "take last place and be the servant of everyone else."[13]

Robert K. Greenleaf, the man who coined the phrase "servant leadership" once said,

> **The servant-leader is servant first. . . . It begins with the natural feeling that one wants to serve, to serve first. Then conscious choice brings one to aspire to lead. That person is sharply different from one who is leader first, perhaps because of the need to assuage an unusual power drive or to acquire material possessions. . . . The leader-first and the servant-first are two extreme types.[14]**

Servanthood is not just a season; it's a lifestyle. The towel you use to wash the feet of the people around you should never become only a reminder of where you started. It needs to be a daily prompt to continue serving. No matter where you are in ministry, what position you hold, or how many people you lead, that towel needs to be tied around your waist at all times.

It's not an easy choice to serve. The Bible tells us,

> **The sinful nature wants to do evil, which is just the opposite of what the Spirit wants. And the Spirit gives us desires that are the opposite of what the sinful nature desires. These two forces are constantly fighting each other, so you are not free to carry out your good intentions.**[15]

Even as followers of Christ, we constantly have to choose to do things that are contrary to the desires of our flesh because we're still human. Some of those desires can seem innocent enough in terms of what we imagine ministry to be: the stage, large crowds, a social media following. But what's the motivation? If you're pursuing ministry to gain power or popularity or influence for yourself, you are a leader-first leader.

According to Greenleaf, the difference between the two types is that a servant-first leader prioritizes the needs of others above anything else. "The best test, and difficult to administer, is: Do those served grow as persons? Do they, while being served, become healthier, wiser, freer, more autonomous, more likely themselves to become servants?"[16]

Ministry can be directed to stadiums full of people, speaking on huge stages, and having millions of YouTube subscribers, but ministry is usually things like making house calls, visiting hospital rooms, stacking chairs, and being assigned to the clean-up crew. It's making sure we are encouraging and loving people. It's about putting the interests of others above our own. It is serving the people in our communities, those leading us, and those under our leadership. It is both taught *and* modeled for us by the Savior of the world, the One who should have His feet washed instead of washing the feet of everyone else.

It is both taught *and* modeled for us by the Savior of the world, the One who should have His feet washed instead of washing the feet of everyone else.

Rev. Martin Luther King, Jr.

So, as you begin this journey, it's important to look to Jesus' example and adopt an others-focused mindset. Rev. Martin Luther King, Jr., once said: "Life's most persistent and urgent question is, 'What are you doing for others?' "[17] Ask yourself that question every day and remember: **No one has ever become poor by serving.**

MAKE IT PLAIN

Every year in November, my parents loaded up all five kids and we would head downtown to serve a Thanksgiving meal to the homeless in our community. Although I wish I could say I loved it and looked forward to this day each year, that wasn't the case. I hated waking up early and I wondered why I had to serve people I didn't know. However, as I got older my perspective – and my heart – changed. Seeing the joy and gratitude of the people we were serving showed me that even though I saw what we were doing as a small gesture, it actually made a significant impact on their lives year after year. It ended up becoming a highlight of Thanksgiving for me!

The Bible teaches us this idea that "it is more blessed to give than to receive."[18] In his commentary, theologian and Bible scholar Adam Clarke said, "A truly generous mind . . . . rejoices in opportunities to do good, and feels happy in having such opportunities."[19] I know this to be true because I experienced it myself: The more I served, the more enjoyable it became. Let me remind you again that Jesus said, "The greatest among you must be a servant."[20]

Serving is an opportunity to do good and will open doors in your ministry that talent and ability cannot and never will. So, find ways to start serving now! Many people make the mistake of waiting until they *feel* qualified, either by earning a degree, gaining more experience, or building a larger following. It's easy to go through the motions – wake up, go to school, come home, eat dinner, go to bed, repeat – until you reach the place you feel like you're "supposed" to be before doing anything.

But where's the fulfillment in that? What if you never get to that place because Jesus wants to take you somewhere else? What if He's waiting to open doors of opportunity until *you* take the first step toward being others-focused? If you don't know where to start, begin with the mindset of doing something for someone else without expecting anything in return. You'll be surprised what the Lord does and where He leads you just by taking that first step in obedience!

It's important to develop a life philosophy of being the same person in public as you are in private in word, deed, and motives.

Here are three areas in your life you can start serving now:

Home – The perfect place to start is in your home, serving the people you live with! It's important to develop a life philosophy of being the same person in public as you are in private in word, deed, and motives. This principle is addressed in 1 Timothy.

Paul wrote about the qualifications expected of church leaders in the Early Church. He said, "[A church leader] must manage his own family well, having children who respect and obey him. For if a man cannot manage his own household, how can he take care of God's church?"[21]

Essentially Paul was saying that if leaders can't lead their own families well, then they shouldn't be given a leadership role in the church. It's crucial that we model integrity in our lives – that the way we live matches what we preach to others.

Here are some practical ideas on how to begin serving in your home:

- Clean your room
- Wash and fold the laundry
- Take out the trash
- Mow the lawn
- Clean the bathroom (I know! This one would be hard for me too!)

Church – Is the church perfect? No, because it's filled with and run by flawed and imperfect people. But that doesn't mean Jesus doesn't love the church with a deep, sacrificial love – He gave up His life for it! We see this is Ephesians when Paul wrote, "For husbands, this means love your wives, just as Christ loved the church. *He gave up his life for her.*"[22]

Even before He went to the Cross, Jesus modeled service to the church when He washed the disciples' feet because it's *people* who make up the church. **Jesus sought to serve rather than be served.[23] We should follow His example, looking to serve the organization God has chosen to accomplish His mission on earth any way we can!**

Here are some practical ideas on how to begin serving in your local church:

- Greet visitors
- Set up for services and events
- Clean up trash
- Serve in an area of interest: children's ministry, media team, worship team, etc.

Community – Many agree that people are creatures of habit. It's easy to set routines, establish habits, and stay within our comfort zones. But sometimes those things can hold us back from what's really important. The community God has placed you in is a mission field. You have opportunities right outside your door to be the hands and feet of Jesus, serving the people He has around you.

You have opportunities right outside your door to be the hands and feet of Jesus, serving the people He has around you.

Feeding the hungry, clothing the naked, caring for the sick – the Bible tells us that whatever we do "to one of the least of these," we are doing to Jesus![24]

Rev. John Wesley

Evangelist and theologian John Wesley once said, "One of the principal rules of religion is, to lose no occasion of serving God. And, since he is invisible to our eyes, we are to serve him in our neighbour; which he receives as if done to himself in person, standing visibly before us."[25]

Choose to start where you are with what you have, serving the people standing in front of you in love, compassion, and humility. Here are some practical ideas on how to begin serving your community:

- Start a Bible club on your school campus
- Organize a food or clothing drive
- Clean up your local parks
- Offer a free car wash
- Volunteer to read aloud to others at the library

True leadership is not about power, position, or authority; it's all about serving. Jesus led by example, and we should model our lives and leadership after Him. By putting the needs of others before your own, you are not only enriching their lives, but you are growing your faith as well.

So, tie that towel around your waist and get to washing!

Take some time to answer the following questions and share them with someone you trust!

1. From this chapter, what stuck out to you the most and why?

2. What is the importance of maintaining the posture of a servant?

3. Do you see places in your life where you tend to be more self-centered? How can you change or fix that?

4. What are some specific ways you can be obedient to God and start serving in these three areas (home, church, community)?

Check out more resources regarding servanthood at:

called.ag.org

Notes

1 Matthew 26:17–30; Mark 14:12–25; Luke 22:7–39; John 13:1–30.
2 John 13:1–17.
3 Mark 10:42–45, emphasis added.
4 J. K. Maner and C. R. Case, "The essential tension between leadership and power," accessed November 13, 2020, https://www.apa.org/science/about/psa/2013/10/leadership-power.
5 T. Sindell and M. Sindell, "The Golden Rule of Leadership," accessed November 13, 2020, https://www.psychologytoday.com/us/blog/the-end-work-you-know-it/201306/the-golden-rule-leadership.
6 Matthew 23:11.
7 Ezekiel 28:12–14.
8 Isaiah 14:12–14.
9 1 Peter 4:10.
10 Philippians 2:3–4.
11 Galatians 5:13–14.
12 Mark 9:35.
13 Robert K. Greenleaf, "What is Servant Leadership?" (n.d.), accessed November 19, 2020, https://www.greenleaf.org/what-is-servant-leadership.
14 Galatians 5:17.
15 Greenleaf, "What is Servant Leadership?"
16 Martin Luther King, Jr., *Strength to Love* (Minneapolis, MN: Fortress Press; Gift edition 2010), 22.
17 Acts 20:35.
18 Adam Clarke, "Commentary on Acts 20:35," *The Adam Clarke Commentary*, accessed November 13, 2020, https://www.studylight.org/commentaries/acc/acts-20.html.
19 Matthew 23:11.
20 1 Timothy 3:4–5.
21 Ephesians 5:25, emphasis added.
22 Matthew 20:28.
23 Matthew 25:40.
24 John Wesley, *A Plain Account of Christian Perfection* (CreateSpace Independent Publishing Platform,), accessed February 19, 2021, https://www.worldinvisible.com/library/wesley/8317/831711.htm.

CHAPTER THREE
SEEK COMMUNITY

Helen Keller

Helen Keller once said, "Alone we can do so little; together we can do so much."[1]

Seems like simple math, right? That's because it is!

God wired humans for community, which is why it makes sense that we can accomplish more together. It doesn't matter whether you're introverted or extroverted, a 2 or an 8 on the Enneagram, or possess the restorative or intellection strength in StrengthsFinder – something within each and every person desires to be part of a community. Throughout the Bible we are taught and reminded of this idea that we need other people. In fact, Ecclesiastes says it like this: "A person standing alone can be attacked and defeated, but two can stand back-to-back and conquer. Three are even better, for a triple-braided cord is not easily broken."[2]

I love hearing messages on this Scripture mostly because the illustrations are so intriguing! One I've used myself goes like this: The speaker starts with one single piece of string and asks someone from the audience to try and rip the string in half. Usually they pick the youngest, smallest, scrawniest student who comes up ready to prove themselves, and they do – the string rips right in half with barely any effort! (The string may or may not have been cut beforehand to ensure it ripped, but no one needs to know that.)

Then, the same speaker calls up the oldest, strongest senior. No one has any doubt that he's going to succeed, especially after seeing what happened the first time around. This time, though, three pieces of string are intertwined. Try as he might, the braid does not rip.

The triple-braided string has a strength that the single piece of string does not.

The triple-braided string has a strength that the single piece of string does not. It may sound like a simple illustration, but through it we can see that since the beginning we were created and designed for community. Try as we might, we cannot ***cover the earth*** going solo with the gospel of Jesus.

The first two chapters of Genesis tell the creation story. The first chapter looks at the creation of the earth – the land, seas, sky, and animals – while the second chapter describes how God formed man from the dust of the earth and breathed life into his body.[3] God and man were in perfect relationship during this time. God planted a garden in Eden, a beautiful environment untainted by sin and brokenness, where He placed the man to care for it. Here God said, "It is not good for the man to be alone. I will make a helper who is just right for him."[4] Then, bringing forth all of the animals and birds, God waited to see what man would name them. Can you imagine being so close to the Creator that the two of you hang out in the Garden of Eden naming animals together?

Despite walking together and talking together, God knew His creation needed to be in meaningful relationships with other human beings. And that's okay! He made it so we would need each other if we were going to make it through this life on earth. He made it so we would need help to accomplish great things. He designed us to be better together!

My early years in ministry were spent at the Assemblies of God Northern California / Nevada district office. I had the honor and privilege of working with several people who mentored me and helped to shape who I am as a leader and a person – then and to this day!

Rev. Sam Huddleston

One person I spent time with during these formative years was assistant superintendent Sam Huddleston. Do you want to know the one thing that has stuck with me all this time? His humility. He often said this: "If you find a turtle sitting on top of a fencepost, you know he didn't get there by himself. Someone had to have helped him get there."

Sam Huddleston made it a point to remember that he – the turtle – didn't get to where he was solely because of what he had done. Countless people played important, valuable roles in his life and were crucial in helping him accomplish his God-given dreams.

We should strive to be like a turtle. We should never get to a place where we look back and applaud ourselves for what we've accomplished. We should never pat ourselves on the back and act as if we accomplished everything on our own, all while pushing people aside or walking over them.

We should never get to a place where we look back and applaud ourselves for what we've accomplished.

We *should* have the humility and wisdom to look back and recognize, "I've been places I shouldn't have been. I've had incredible opportunities that I shouldn't have had. And I couldn't have done any of it without the person who encouraged me, the person who gave me a chance, and the person who didn't give up on me."

So, we've established that relationships are essential, but we have to be very intentional in surrounding ourselves with people who will help us fulfill God's purpose for our lives. Have you ever heard the saying, "Show me your friends and I'll show you your future"? Well, the Bible says it like this: "Walk with the wise and become wise; associate with fools and get in trouble."[5]

I'm not talking about spending time with smart people instead of spending time with the class clowns. But wise men and women think before they speak. They are humble and peaceable. They accept instruction and correction. Bible scholar Joseph Exell said this in commenting on Proverbs 13:20:

> **A wise man is one who proposes to himself the most valuable ends, and pursues them by the best means. A fool is one who either has no worthy ends in view, or does not pursue them by proper means. The prudent is the wise man. The inconsiderate is the fool. The wise man is the true believer and holy soul; and the fool is the impenitent sinner, who rejects Christ and His salvation.[6]**

The Bible warns against spending time with foolish people because it's human nature to imitate others.[7] **Often, we imitate unconsciously which is why we must take extra precautions and be intentional and purposeful about who we surround ourselves with.**

Knowing we all imitate others without thinking, why would we choose to spend time with inconsiderate, lazy, or selfish people when we could be around those who can help us look more like Jesus? I'm not saying you can't be friends with certain people or show them love and care; it's more about who you are giving permission to speak into your life. You should want to have people in your life who are going to develop, encourage, and stretch you!

Now, it's important to distinguish between "communities" and "networks." We've established that humans were created for community. God designed us in a way that we would need one another. However, our culture today often emphasizes "networks," "networking," or "building your network." Nothing is inherently wrong with that sentiment, but a negative connotation can accompany it.

People often see or understand networking as manipulation to get to the top, building relationships with titles and positions, rather than people who can give us what we need to move higher and faster. That mindset is selfish and greedy, and it's not the heart of God. **We need to prioritize building and investing in genuine relationships, in other words, *community*.**

Let's go back to Genesis 2, where we read that after God placed the man in the Garden of Eden, He warned him:

"You may freely eat the fruit of every tree in the garden – except the tree of the knowledge of good and evil. If you eat its fruit, you are sure to die."[8]

Adam and Eve

Immediately after giving the man his first command, God then said it was not good for him to be alone. Isn't that interesting? God knew from the very beginning that community was fundamental for us; we need relationship and accountability with others if we are to live according to His Word.

One common saying goes like this: "If you want to go quickly, go alone. If you want to go far, go together." As people who are called into ministry, our goal should not be perfection, fame, or wealth; it should be to lead with love, integrity, and purity of heart. To do that, we need to commit to being a part of a group, connecting with and holding each other accountable. **We need to be open to allowing the people who will develop, encourage, and stretch us to address areas of strength and weakness.** We need to resist isolating ourselves from community and be intentional about challenging the lie that we can do it on our own.

God knew from the very beginning that community was fundamental for us; we need relationship and accountability with others if we are to live according to His Word.

First John tells us, "But if we are living in the light, as God is in the light, then we have fellowship with each other, and the blood of Jesus, his Son, cleanses us from all sin."[9] God had a reason for saying He would create a helper for man: When we walk with Him, healthy, strong, and lasting relationships with other people are a natural result.

We'll go much further when we accept and act on the knowledge that we genuinely, sincerely need other people.

MAKE IT PLAIN

You should pursue these three key relationships as you seek to build your community: someone to *develop* you, someone to *encourage* you, and someone to *stretch* you. Rather than expecting others to act first and seek you out, make a decision to prayerfully consider who *you* should invite to fill these roles.

Develop – Paul was a spiritual father to many believers in the Early Church, one of whom was a man named Timothy. The New Testament books of 1 and 2 Timothy were letters written by Paul to Timothy regarding his ministry in the city of Ephesus. Paul chose to intentionally invest in the life of the young believer. As a young person following the call of ministry on your life, seek out spiritual mentors who will invest in your life as well.

According to Merriam-Webster, the word *mentor* is often used "for anyone who is a positive, guiding influence in another (usually younger) person's life."[10] **Mentorship is a valuable relationship necessary for growth. Mentors can look different for different people** – a pastor, a teacher, a sibling, a friend. What's important is finding someone who is spiritually mature, possesses relevant knowledge and wisdom, has the capacity and desire to invest in others, and will encourage and challenge the mentee to grow in their own faith journey.

You can have a **distant mentor** – someone you follow from afar. You may have never met this person, but you admire their character and ministry approach. You can still learn from this mentor by listening to and observing them, and reading and studying their works. You can even learn by reading and listening to how other people talk about them. Even if you never have the opportunity to meet a distant mentor face-to-face, you can make the choice to allow them to develop who you are as a person and a leader.

You can have **near mentors** – people you talk to periodically. You trust their wisdom, advice, and insight, but maybe only seek them out during specific situations or seasons. That's okay! Not every mentor has to have unlimited access to you and your life. Interactions with near mentors don't have to be daily, weekly, or even monthly, but when you do connect, their experience and knowledge can help guide you.

Not every mentor has to have unlimited access to you and your life.

Then you will want **close mentors** – people in your inner circle. These are people you completely trust, and have given permission to know you inside and out, as well as to speak into your life on a regular basis. These relationships are unique in that they take thought, time, and effort on *both* sides. Not only does the mentor have a responsibility to guide you when they accept your invitation, but you also have a responsibility to engage with and show you want to learn from this person. **Communication is key; you should be transparent and honest with a close mentor in order for their direction and feedback to really make a difference in your life.**

Shannon Sullivan

In sixth grade, I was involved in my youth group for only a few months before I found a leader I wanted to be like – Shannon Sullivan. I approached Shannon one night after service at my first-ever district youth convention. For context, remember the small, scrawny kid I mentioned at the beginning of this chapter? That was me!

The way Shannon tells the story is that some small kid with shaggy hair and a squeaky voice walked up and asked him, "Hey, can I have a Bible study at your house with me and some of my friends? And you can like, mentor us?" He says from that moment on I have never stopped showing up at his house and eating his food.

Eighteen years later I can confidently and humbly say Shannon is the closest mentor in my life, not only because he accepted the responsibility to mentor me, but because

I also still choose to show up. I know I would not be who I am and where I'm at without his investment in my life. Even though I sought him out at first, it has been a God-ordained relationship.

Many times we wait for someone to seek us and ask to be our mentor. That can happen, but we shouldn't sit back and wait for it.

Many times we wait for someone to seek us and ask to be our mentor. That can happen, but we shouldn't sit back and wait for it. Even if you feel weird or hesitant, like a puny, awkward sixth-grader, you might be surprised at how God moves when you seek out your Paul.

Encourage – Another important character in the Bible is Barnabas. We first hear about him in the Book of Acts: "For instance, there was Joseph, the one the apostles nicknamed Barnabas (which means 'Son of Encouragement'). He was from the tribe of Levi and came from the island of Cyprus."[11]

We learn early on that Barnabas was an encourager – so much so that it became his name! In Acts 9, we read about how Paul tried to meet with other believers, but people were afraid of him because of his history of persecuting Christians.[12] Barnabas vouched for Paul's transformation, and Paul "stayed with the apostles and went all around Jerusalem with them, preaching boldly in the name of the Lord."[13] Barnabas's support and encouragement in Paul's life helped to grow and mature Paul's ministry. He and Paul worked alongside each other, ***covering the earth*** with the gospel.

The second area of community you need to invest in is friendships. We all need a Barnabas-type friend to do life with. If I were to ask you what traits you would find in a "perfect" friend, I'm sure we would agree on the list. An article in *Psychology Today* asked the same question and identifies these seven traits: empathetic, selfless, trustworthy, humorous, team players, have shared interests, and have different perspectives and backgrounds.[14]

Think about these traits in relation to your friendships. Think about the friends you can totally be yourself with: the ones you can text whenever and they'll always respond; the ones you go to when you need a listening ear, a wise word, or a moment of laughter. Who of these friends has your best interest at heart and pushes you to be a better version of yourself?

The Bible tells us, "As iron sharpens iron, so a friend sharpens a friend."[15] Sharpening is a process used to create or refine a sharp edge on a tool, so the phrase "iron sharpening iron" suggests we need two pieces of iron for the process to be effective. In the same way, two believers can sharpen each other to help them both grown stronger in their faith. **We need people in our community who can and want to help us get better.** We need people who are willing to be vulnerable and have hard conversations. We need people who challenge us not because they want to be harsh or critical, but because it will help us grow closer to one another and to God.

Finding your iron sounds simple, but it's not easy. There's a difference between knowing we are better when we have strong, healthy relationships with other people, and actually making an effort to build those relationships. That's why I have a reminder in my phone (see how that discipline continues to show up in my life?) to call or text my "irons." I also have a once-a-month call set up with my Barnabas. It's a chance for both of us to be completely honest and open about where we are at – struggles, victories, prayer requests. We then take time to process those things, encourage each other, and pray together.

I notice I seem to have a hard time making that call to my Barnabas every month though. I have to be willing to show a level of vulnerability to share my areas of weakness with him. I have to find the motivation to call in the seasons where I feel too busy to set aside time to talk. Relationships are a two-way street, so I also have to make a commitment to invest in him and hold him accountable.

But, every time I hang up the phone, I feel like a million bucks! I feel seen, understood, and supported which confirms the knowledge that God created us for community. Again, finding your Barnabas may not come easily, but it will make your life so much better!

Stretch – The third and final relationship to seek out is your Timothy. Once again, Timothy was the young disciple who received a life-changing investment from Paul. The older man saw potential in Timothy and decided it was worth the time and effort to mentor him. Paul prayed for Timothy day and night.[16] He also encouraged Timothy to use the gifts God had given him and challenged him to never be ashamed of the gospel.[17] Paul wanted Timothy to stay committed to his calling in order to grow into the effective leader Paul knew he could be.

We have a unique opportunity in ministry to lead and strategically invest in others like Paul did for Timothy. Their relationship is a powerful example of how we may benefit from mentors, but God also wants us to *be* a mentor for others. So, whose Paul can you be?

We have a unique opportunity in ministry to lead and strategically invest in others like Paul did for Timothy.

The answer to this question may take some time and prayer to determine. Before anything else, you need to be in a mentally, emotionally, and spiritually sound place in order to teach someone else. You also need to be honest with yourself about the commitment mentoring someone else will be. Do you have the capacity and desire to commit to that relationship at this time? There's no right or wrong answer; just determine what God is speaking to you.

Now, that's not to say you can get away without ever mentoring someone else – especially as a ministry leader – but you need to exercise wisdom in this area of your community. More than anything in this "stretch" area, the goal is your mentee's success. It's not about you, but about what you can do to help the turtle get to the top of the fencepost.

Actor Denzel Washington made a powerful statement on mentorship:

> **Show me a successful individual and I'll show you someone who had real positive influences in his or her life. I don't care what you do for a living—if you do it well, I'm sure there was someone cheering you on or showing the way. A mentor."[18]**

Some of the relationships you build will last the rest of your life, like my relationship with Shannon. Other relationships may be necessary for only a season. When I started out in ministry, I had a mentor who played a vital role in my life for a period of time. When that season ended, my relationship with this person shifted and I no longer considered them a mentor. Neither one of us did anything wrong; God had just placed them in my life for a season and that's okay.

Again, pray about each area. Pray for God to bring people to mind you would like to be mentored by and ask for wisdom on how to approach that conversation. Pray for those people you will have the opportunity to mentor someday. Don't rush into anything – these are valuable relationships that deserve thoughtful consideration. God will help you build a strong, healthy community as you seek meaningful relationships with Him and with others.

Take some time to answer the following questions and share them with someone you trust.

1. From this chapter, what stuck out to you the most and why?

2. Do you find it difficult to ask for help? Why or why not?

3. Do you enjoy helping others succeed? Why or why not?

4. Prayerfully consider who you might want to ask to fill each of these roles in your life.

Check out more resources regarding seeking community at:

called.ag.org

Notes

1 Joseph P. Lash, *Helen and Teacher: The Story of Helen Keller and Anne Sullivan Macy* (Lawrence, NY: Delacorte Press/Seymour, 1980), 489.

2 Ecclesiastes 4:12.

3 Genesis 2:7.

4 Genesis 2:18.

5 Proverbs 13:20.

6 Joseph S. Exell, "Commentary on Proverbs 13:20," *The Biblical Illustrator*, New York, 1905-1909, accessed December 4, 2020, https://www.studylight.org/commentaries/tbi/proverbs-13.html.

7 Alain Sampson, "Copy That," *Psychology Today*, April 11, 2012, accessed December 4, 2020, https://www.psychologytoday.com/us/blog/consumed/201204/copy.

8 Genesis 2:16–17.

9 1 John 1:7.

10 *Merriam-Webster.com Dictionary*, s.v. "mentor," accessed December 10, 2020, https://www.merriam-webster.com/dictionary/mentor.

11 Acts 4:36.

12 Acts 9:26–27.

13 Acts 9:28.

14 Greta Gleissner, "7 Traits of True Friendship," *Psychology Today* (October 27, 2016), accessed December 11, 2020, https://www.psychologytoday.com/us/blog/bottoms/201610/7-traits-true-friendship.

15 Proverbs 27:17.

16 2 Timothy 1:3.

17 2 Timothy 1:6–8.

18 Denzel Washington, "The Mentors He'll Never Forget," *Guideposts* (January 1, 2007), accessed February 9, 2021, https://www.guideposts.org/better-living/positive-living/the-mentors-hell-never-forget.

CHAPTER FOUR
DISCOVER GIFTS

You made all the delicate, inner parts of my body and knit me together in my mother's womb. Thank you for making me so wonderfully complex! Your workmanship is marvelous—how well I know it.[1]

The Psalmist uses so much description in his words about how God purposefully and intentionally creates each new life. **God intricately designs every detail of our being, knitting us together in our mother's womb. The Psalmist cannot help but praise Him.**

Sometimes I wonder why the Psalmist used the word *knit*. The Creator of the universe knows us, sees us, and shapes us in a way no one else can, so why not describe that process as something like *forged*, *sculpted*, or *crafted*?

I have never knitted before, but I know it requires focus, patience, persistence, and *a lot* of practice. Knitting uses different types of stitches and stitch patterns, a variety of knitting needles, and countless yarn options. All those options create just as many ways to make a mistake on a project. That's why someone who knits has to pay attention to what they're doing – running on autopilot may lead to dropping or missing some stitches, which then takes additional time and effort to fix. Knitting is an activity that takes special attention to detail and, depending on the type of project, hours upon hours of dedication and perseverance.

He knows exactly why He creates each unique individual and exactly what He creates them for.

The reason why this word *knit* is used to describe how God created you may be because He paid very special attention to what He was doing. He doesn't use a template to create copies of people – He knows exactly why He creates each unique individual and exactly what He creates them for. That's true for *you*! When He created you, He focused on stringing together your DNA. He intentionally formed your physical attributes. And He planned for your future with each gift He placed in you.

In the last chapter, we discussed the truth that God created us for community, but that's not the only reason we were created. He gives us gifts – different abilities, talents, passions – which are tools He wants us to use to fulfill His plan of ***covering the earth*** with the gospel!

But a specific process accompanies discovering and developing these skills you possess. (And yes, you already have these skills because like the psalm says, God knit you together with those in mind!) This process will take time, sometimes your whole life, as you discover and continually hone your various talents and abilities. It may take trial and error. You may try something you didn't think you would like and realize that you're actually really good at it and enjoy it! And then there will be things you thought you would like or be good at, but it didn't turn out how you expected.

That thought may excite some of you and intimidate others, and that's okay! Neither feeling is wrong. **You have so much to offer God, your family and friends, and this world, but the first step of realizing those gifts and potential lies in your willingness to let God use what you have no matter if it ends in success or failure.**

When I was in eighth grade, I thought it would be fun to try out for band. Now, let me tell you I don't have a musical bone in my body. Just ask anyone who stands next to me during a worship service! I like to think my singing is filtered by the clouds before it reaches heaven, making it a joyful noise in the ears of the Lord. But why not at least try it?

I started to think music wasn't for me as I tried instrument after instrument and kept failing miserably – until I found the drums. I thought this was it! Boy, was I wrong. In the middle of practice one day, the band instructor stopped everyone and said, "If one person is off the beat, we're all off. I'm not going to say names, but the blond-haired kid on the drums in the back is throwing the whole thing off." (By the way, I have blond hair.) Also, I found out I'm tone deaf, so that was my last year of band.

> **It's important that you don't get discouraged in your journey either, because God chose *you* and gave *you* specific talents and gifts.**

I could have been discouraged, frustrated, or embarrassed, but actually I'm glad I went through that experience. I'm glad discovering our God-given gifts is a process. It's important that you don't get discouraged in your journey either, because God chose *you* and gave *you* specific talents and gifts.

The process of discovering and developing those gifts is about exactly that. As believers we need to take a step further and recognize the process is also about how to develop those gifts in a way that honors God. Author Neil T. Anderson wrote, **"Fulfillment is discovering our own uniqueness in Christ and using our gifts and talents to edify others and to glorify the Lord."**[2]

David

One man we read about in the Bible is David. Most of us know him from when he defeated the Philistine giant Goliath with just a slingshot and a stone,[3] but we often pass over other details of David's life like his harp playing.

David was anointed to be the king of Israel as a young shepherd boy[4] but his harp brought him into the throne room long before he stepped into that calling. Scripture tells us that the Spirit of the Lord came upon David on the day of his anointing.

The Spirit of the Lord had left King Saul. The Lord sent a "tormenting spirit that filled him with depression and fear."[5]

One of Saul's servants offered to find someone to play the harp to soothe Saul whenever the spirit was tormenting him. That musician was David, and "whenever the tormenting spirit from God troubled Saul, David would play the harp. Then Saul would feel better, and the tormenting spirit would go away."[6]

This wasn't the only time David used his gifts to glorify God. One writer states, "The anointing upon his musical gift called warriors to battle and brought peace. His prophetic songs of joyful praise and warfare worship ring out in churches yet today, proclaiming the greatness, goodness and faithfulness of God."[7] **God knit this gift into David's DNA knowing it would help him accomplish what he was created to do. The many hours David spent playing his instrument, writing poetry and music, and worshipping became part of the discovery process.**

What has God knit in you that will help you accomplish what you were created to do? If you read that question and you don't know, or are unsure of the answer, here are a few questions to ask yourself *before* you answer this first question.

- What am I naturally good at?
- What do people around me say I am good at?
- What do I love to do that I would do for free?

Answering these questions probably won't give you 100 percent clarity or direction when it comes to discovering your gifts, but it's a start!

To experience the discovery process in its entirety, you must be dedicated to honest reflection. Be dedicated to growth. Be dedicated to trial and error. Be dedicated to setting goals. Be dedicated to improvement and persistence. Be dedicated to *trusting the process*. And, like Anderson stated, you will find fulfillment when you discover your own uniqueness in Christ and use your gifts and talents to glorify God.

To experience the discovery process in its entirety, you must be dedicated to honest reflection.

Scripture echoes this thought in Colossians when it says, "Work willingly at whatever you do, as though you were working for the Lord rather than for people."[8] While this verse applies to all believers, it is especially true for those who have felt the call to vocational ministry. Whatever type of ministry you feel called to – pastor, church planter, missionary, or evangelist – work at it with all your heart as if you were working for the Lord, because you are!

In the introduction we talked about the body of Christ.[9] This passage tells us how God created us all with unique talents and abilities to fulfill our distinct purpose. While we all have a responsibility to ***cover the earth*** with the gospel, we are called to accomplish that in different ways according to the God-given gifts we have. My gifts and your gifts are part of a bigger picture. **When everyone is working in their giftings, we see God's intentional design at work.** And because we're not all created the same, we don't have to compete. Instead, we *complement* one another and work best when we work together.

We can see this idea play out in team sports; when you are on a team, you are not competing against your teammate. You have to work in your position and recognize the value and necessity of other positions to score or prevent the other team from scoring.

Two players on the Golden State Warriors basketball team understand this concept. Steph Curry and Klay Thompson are two of the greatest shooters of all time. These two players are not threatened by each other's abilities. Instead, they value each other's skills and work to be better as a team.

Steph Curry

A video clip of Curry and Thompson from a game on February 6, 2019, against the San Antonio Spurs is a perfect example of what complementing each other actually looks like.[10] Both Curry and Thompson were wide open outside the three-point line as a teammate looked to pass the ball. But instead of calling for it himself, each player pointed to the other as if to say, "He's open, pass *him* the ball!" The example Curry and Thompson set not only illustrates how our different gifts, talents, and skills can be used to complement each other, but it shows selflessness, humility, and confidence in other people's abilities.

This shouldn't just be limited to team sports. This is how we should be operating as the Church! Like the passage in 1 Corinthians says, to function properly we need each member to do their part. **It's beneficial for people to operate in their unique giftings and roles as well as for the body of Christ as a whole. And it's critical that we recognize the value and importance of the gifts that other people have and then cooperate with them.**

Instead of exhibiting jealousy of other gifts, being discontent with the role God has you in, or displaying pride in your own abilities, think about this: "God has given each of you a gift from his great variety of spiritual gifts. Use them well to *serve one another*."[11] Our gifts are not tools to build our own personal platforms. Our gifts are tools we can use to glorify the Creator who gave them to us and to edify others.

Imagine the ministry effectiveness we as believers would have if we simply appreciated all of the diverse talents, skills, and abilities God has given His people, whether we possess the same ones or not. Pastor and author Rick Warren once wrote something similar: "Your spiritual gifts were not given for your own benefit but for the benefit of others, just as other people were given gifts for your benefit."[12]

There's no need for comparison in the body of Christ. You will never be able to appreciate the God-given gifts others have until you fully embrace your own. That is why intentionally taking the time to discover your specific skill sets and abilities is for you *and* the Church. As you learn, grow, and improve, a natural byproduct is confidence – not confidence in what you can do, but in what you know God can do through you. When we each understand that idea and *truly* believe it, we can work together as God intended it to ***cover the earth*** with the love of Jesus.

> **There's no need for comparison in the body of Christ. You will never be able to appreciate the God-given gifts others have until you fully embrace your own.**

MAKE IT PLAIN

As we've covered in this chapter, each person is knitted together by God with different abilities to fulfill their calling. **While discovering our gifts benefits us and allows us to honor God in our personal faith journeys, the body of Christ functions best when we work together.**

In the Book of Ephesians, Paul writes about five ministry roles in the church: apostle, prophet, evangelist, pastor, and teacher. He gives us a blueprint to equip and serve others and grow the Church.

> **Now these are the gifts Christ gave to the church: the apostles, the prophets, the evangelists, and the**

pastors and teachers. Their responsibility is to equip God's people to do his work and build up the church, the body of Christ. This will continue until we all come to such unity in our faith and knowledge of God's Son that we will be mature in the Lord, measuring up to the full and complete standard of Christ.

Then we will no longer be immature like children. We won't be tossed and blown about by every wind of new teaching. We will not be influenced when people try to trick us with lies so clever they sound like the truth. Instead, we will speak the truth in love, growing in every way more and more like Christ, who is the head of his body, the church. He makes the whole body fit together perfectly. As each part does its own special work, it helps the other parts grow, so that the whole body is healthy and growing and full of love.[13]

Another help as you begin to discover your ministry calling is to take a simple assessment about the five spiritual gifts. It's commonly thought that we all have a strong bent toward one or two of these areas. Even though we may possess the same gift as another believer, more than likely it will manifest in a different way in our lives. That's why it's so important to discover your own giftings through things like self-reflection, trial and error, and setting goals.

Use the link on the called.ag.org website for a free test[14] that can help you begin to determine what your natural bent is. The short descriptions for the five spiritual gifts on the test are included below with descriptors created by J. R. Woodward.

Apostle

People who score highest for an apostolic position are Dream Awakeners[15] in the kingdom of God. They awaken people to their God-designed potential. They are instrumental in helping people discover who they really are and walking alongside them to get there. They forge new paths in the Kingdom and are a catalyst for change wherever they go.

Prophet

People who score highest for a prophetic position are Heart Revealers[16] in the kingdom of God. They are effective in revealing God's heart for His people. They can accurately discern God's heart for a situation. They help people experience God's voice for the very first time and help them develop the skill of hearing the voice of God in their own life.

Evangelist

People who score highest for an evangelist position are Story Tellers[17] in the kingdom of God. They make the stories of Jesus' remarkable goodness and love famous. They are a carrier of good news and partner with Jesus in celebrating people's transformation. They stir curiosity and desire to know Jesus. Their life is a living invitation to all to join the family of God.

Pastor

People who score highest for a pastoral position are Soul Healers[18] in the kingdom of God. They are instrumental in guiding people through brokenness back to wholeness and healing their soul from wounds that keep them where they are. They create a safe atmosphere of family and belonging. They bring fun and enjoyment to God's ministry and allow people to feel like they are part of a greater family.

Teacher

People who score highest for a teaching position are Light Givers[19] in the kingdom of God. They make the truth and knowledge about God accessible to all. They have an ability for breaking confusion and misinformation. They are strategic in helping people know the truth of God and also how it applies to their own life.

My main gift is as an apostle followed by pastor. Incredibly, I can see how my skills and abilities align with these roles. I am passionate about awakening people to their God-designed potential. I love to listen to others' stories. I have a knack for identifying strengths and weaknesses in others. And I desire to see others succeed and walk in the calling God has upon their life. I only tell you this because I want you to understand that you have the same potential within you, too!

Let's think about a glow stick. When you buy a glow stick, **you don't have to go back to the manufacturer and ask them to add the chemicals to make it shine for you.** Every chemical compound and solution needed for the glow stick to fulfill its purpose is already inside it. The only thing missing is bending and breaking the glow stick.

Similarly, we don't have to go to God and ask Him to instill some gifts in us – He already did that when He knit us together! We can ask for other gifts as well (see 1 Corinthians 12:31). We may not see our talents and skills as tools we can use to build the Church, which is why the discovery process is so crucial in the life of a believer. We may need to be bent and broken, fully submitted to God before realizing that what we needed to fulfill our calling was always within us.

Similarly, we don't have to go to God and ask Him to instill some gifts in us—He already did that when He knit us together!

The church has a need for all the various gifts. That's how God intended it.

We cannot and should not compare our gifts to the gifts of another, nor should we envy what others have. **Every gift you have from God is essential for the body of Christ the same as every gift from God the person next to you has.** God intentionally designed you with the talents, passions, and skills you need to fulfill your part of the mission of ***covering the earth*** with the love of Jesus. Fortunately, you are only responsible for your actions and choices. You are responsible to make sure you do the most with what God has given you.

In Matthew 25, Jesus told a story about a master who, before going on a journey, distributed his wealth among three servants.[20] Some Bible versions talk about bags of silver and some use the word *talent* is used to describe the form of money the master gave the servants. To one servant the master gave five talents, to another he gave two talents, and to the third he gave one talent. Verse 15 tells us that the master gave "dividing it in proportion to their abilities," and then went on his journey.

Bags of Silver

The Bible tells us the servant with five talents worked hard and earned five more, and the servant with two earned two more. However, the servant with one talent hid the master's money in a hole in the ground and didn't do anything with it. When the master returned, he called his servants to give an account for how they used the money. The two who doubled the investment were told, "Well done, my good and faithful servant. You have been faithful in handling this small amount, so now I will give you many more responsibilities. Let's celebrate together!"[21]

Then the servant who hid the master's money in a hole came and said, "Master, I knew you were a harsh man, harvesting crops you didn't plant and gathering crops you didn't cultivate. I was afraid I would lose your money, so I hid it in the earth. Look, here is your money back."[22]

This servant failed the test because he misunderstood the master's heart. It was not about *how many* talents anyone was given; it was about what they *did* with what they were given. The master, who represents God in this story, gave the talents to each servant according to their abilities. He did not give the talents randomly or by chance. But misunderstanding the master can keep a person from discovering what they have in their hand and developing it in a healthy, God-honoring way.

It was not about *how many* talents anyone was given; it was about what they *did* with what they were given.

What will you do with what God has given you? Will you hide it away? Will you compare what you have to what others have? Or will you do your part with what God has given you? Will you take time to discover what is already knitted within you? Will you dedicate time and energy to developing your gifts properly? Then work at whatever you do with all your heart, as if you were working for God (see Colossians 3:23). That's where your greatest fulfillment in life will come from.

Take some time to answer the following questions and share them with someone you trust.

1. From this chapter, what stuck out to you the most and why?

2. What are you naturally good at?

3. What do you love to do? What do you hate to do?

4. Take the spiritual gift test online at called.ag.org and prayerfully consider how God may want to use your gifts for His purpose.

Check out more resources regarding discovering gifts at:

called.ag.org

Notes

1 Psalm 139:13–14.
2 Neil T. Anderson, *Victory Over the Darkness: Realizing the Power of Your Identity in Christ* (Ventura, CA: Regal Book, 2000), 143.
3 1 Samuel 17:1–51.
4 1 Samuel 16:11–13.
5 1 Samuel 16:13–14
6 1 Samuel 16:15–18, 23.
7 Connie Ruth Christiansen, "Worship Music: Lessons from David and His Harp," *Share Faith*, accessed December 23, 2020, https://www.sharefaith.com/guide/Christian-Music/praise-and-worship/david-and-his-harp.html.
8 Colossians 3:23.
9 1 Corinthians 12:12–27.
10 "Steph Curry Klay Thompson pointing play summed up Warriors' selflessness," *NBC Sports* (May 18, 2020), accessed January 2, 2021, https://www.nbcsports.com/bayarea/warriors/steph-curry-klay-thompson-pointing-play-summed-warriors-selflessness.
11 1 Peter 4:10, emphasis added.
12 Rick Warren, *The Purpose-Driven Life: What on Earth Am I Here for?* (Grand Rapids, MI: Zondervan, 2002), 60.
13 Ephesians 4:11–16.
14 called.ag.org.
15 J. R. Woodward, *Creating a Missional Culture: Equipping the Church for the Sake of the World* (Downers Grove, IL: IVP Books, 2012), 123.
16 Woodward, *Creating a Missional Culture*, 131.
17 Woodward, *Creating a Missional Culture*, 141.
18 Woodward, *Creating a Missional Culture*, 150.
19 Woodward, *Creating a Missional Culture*, 160.
20 Matthew 25:14–30.
21 Matthew 25:21, 23.
22 Matthew 25:24–25.

CHAPTER FIVE
LEARN PASSIONS

Have you ever heard the phrase, "holy discontent"? *Merriam-Webster* defines discontent as "lack of satisfaction with one's possessions, status, or situation" or "lack of contentment."[1] But something about this definition changes when you put the word *holy* in front of it.

I have sometimes wondered why people do what they do. Everyone has an underlying motivation about what they choose – the careers they pick, the volunteer opportunities they sign up for, and the causes they donate to. But sometimes we see or experience things that cause something in us to snap. We then say, "That's it. I can't take this anymore!"

***That's* holy discontent—taking the frustration and anger you feel about a certain problem, injustice, or struggle, and using those feelings as motivation to fix that problem or right that wrong.**

Popeye the Sailor Man illustrates this idea. Introduced in 1929, Popeye is a cartoon character who would experience an adventure and conflict, typically involving his love, Olive Oyl. Popeye would endure an enemy's antics as long as he could, but if it seemed like something really terrible might happen to Olive, he would abruptly say, "That's all I can stands, and I can't stands no more!"[2] He would then whip out a can of

spinach and suck it down in one gulp. Almost immediately, his muscles would grow and he would have the supernatural strength to resolve the conflict to his liking and save Olive.

Have you ever experienced a Popeye moment? What causes you to stop and say, "That's all I can stands, and I can't stands no more"?

For many, the motivation to change or fix something in the world came because they saw something wrong. That moment of frustration or anger sparked something within them.

Personally, I have found that some of my biggest passions in life are closely tied to moments of frustration. Sometimes, God works that way. He will use the very things that wreck and disturb us to propel us into action. Even so, you probably won't wake up tomorrow knowing exactly what your number one passion is or how to remedy all the wrongs related to it.

He will use the very things that wreck and disturb us to propel us into action.

Often a process or series of events finally reveals what our holy discontent is. You may be frustrated about a lot of different things and passionate to initiate change, but it's crucial that you view these frustrations from a heavenly perspective. Our God is a God of redemption and restoration, and He invites us to partner with Him in His restoration plan.

Frustration is inevitable, but we get to choose how we respond. Directing your attention to every annoying, irritating thing can become overwhelming and cause you to get stuck in those feelings. But bringing the irritation to God and asking Him to help you see these issues through His point of view can help determine if it is a holy discontent. He can then give direction and fuel your desire to ***cover the earth*** with the love of Jesus.

The Bible tells us about a man who, after operating out of frustration in his own way, partnered with God to use his passion as the driving force in delivering God's people from slavery. Let's look at the story of Moses.

Exodus 1 says that the Israelites multiplied and filled the land of Egypt, outnumbering the Egyptians. A new pharaoh rose to power and was afraid the Israelites would become too powerful and turn against the Egyptians. He forced the Israelites into slavery, but "the more the Egyptians oppressed them, the more the Israelites multiplied and spread, and the more alarmed the Egyptians became."[3] As Pharaoh grew more afraid, he ordered every Hebrew baby boy to be thrown into the Nile River and killed.[4]

A son was born to a Hebrew couple. The mother kept the baby hidden for a few months until she was unable to hide him any longer. Placing the baby in a basket, she floated it in the reeds along the Nile. Pharaoh's daughter found the baby, saved him, and named him Moses. She had compassion on this baby and adopted him as her own son.[5] What a plot twist!

Moses

Although raised as Egyptian royalty, Moses knew he was a Hebrew by birth. He only had the privileges of an Egyptian life because of a chance encounter when he was three months old.

Scripture tells us, "Many years later, when Moses had grown up, he went out to visit his own people, the Hebrews, and he saw how hard they were forced to work. During his visit, he saw an Egyptian beating one of his fellow Hebrews."[6]

The Hebrews lived in a harsh environment and were mistreated every day. It's very likely that Moses saw these conditions throughout his life. But on this day, seeing this Hebrew's abuse was an "I can't stand any more!" moment for Moses. "After looking in all directions to make sure no one was watching, Moses killed the Egyptian and hid the body in the sand."[7]

Yikes! Talk about frustration. But this was not the end of the story – the very next day Moses found out that others knew he had murdered the Egyptian. Fearing for his life, Moses fled from Egypt and lived in the desert for forty years.

One chapter later in Exodus, Moses encountered God at a burning bush. Tending to his flock one day, Moses noticed a bush on fire that was not being consumed. When God saw Moses turn to take a closer look, He spoke. God told Moses that He had heard the cries of the Israelites and was going to rescue them with Moses's help![8]

God called Moses to act out of his passion for his people—to lead them out of Egypt into freedom. Why? Because God knew this was Moses's holy discontent. He couldn't stand by and allow the Israelites to be enslaved and mistreated any longer. God was going to use Moses's frustration to propel him into fulfilling the very purpose he was created for.

Moses isn't the only person in history with a holy discontent. Every single day, men and women are stirred by problems and injustices, passionate to create change and right a myriad of wrongs.

Take Martin Luther King, Jr., for example. As a pastor-turned-civil-rights-leader, he despised the racial tension and oppression all around him during the 1950s and 1960s. The segregation, mistreatment, and murder of African Americans was too much. In effect King said, “That’s all I can stand, and I can’t stand any more!” Participating in and leading marches, King worked toward change. His frustration fueled his passion to see racial reconciliation and equality achieved.

Rosa Parks

At the same time King was entering the national spotlight, Rosa Parks had her own, “I can’t stand any more!” moment. In December 1955, Parks, a civil rights activist herself, was arrested on a Montgomery, Alabama, bus for refusing to give up her seat to a white passenger.

At this time public transportation was segregated, requiring separate but equal seating accommodations – white passengers in the front and African American passengers in the back. As the bus filled with passengers, the driver noticed white people standing in the aisle and stopped the bus. He asked four black passengers to give up their seats, and only three complied. Parks said, “I don’t think I should have to stand up.”[9] Her arrest inspired the Montgomery Bus Boycott – a boycott that lasted 381 days and ended with a Supreme Court ruling that segregation on public transportation was unconstitutional. **Parks' holy discontent changed history.**

Beth Grant, an Assemblies of God missionary, executive presbyter, and founder of Project Rescue (a ministry to restore human trafficking victims), points to Isaiah 59:9–14 in her book *Courageous Compassion*. This passage tells us that God sees injustice in the world and "is appalled" that no one intervenes. She says this:

> **But as in all of Scripture, the reality of the darkness in Isaiah 59 and God's response to it demands a response from His children. God was and is appalled. Are we? Where is the church—God's people—in the face of great spiritual darkness, violence, and injustice? Are we wringing our proverbial hands? Are we declining to comment? Have we lost our God-given voice? Or are we responding in the spirit and example of Jesus, whom we follow? . . . In the face of great darkness and evil, it's time for God's people to stand up![10]**

So, let me ask you again: What issue in the world can't you stand? What problem do you want to see solved? Hal Donaldson, founder of Convoy of Hope, an international organization to bring help and hope to the impoverished, hungry, and hurting, wrote this in his book *Disruptive Compassion*:

> **Change the world? That's an absolute joke if you don't believe in your mission. Seriously, ask yourself if you believe a "better world" is possible. Do you really believe you can play a role in reducing poverty, pollution, abuse, racism, crime, human trafficking, and more?[11]**

On the other hand, if we are not careful our passions can cause anger and bitterness to take root in our heart. **The line between a healthy and an unhealthy frustration is very thin.**

The Bible tells us, "The human heart is the most deceitful of all things, and desperately wicked. Who really knows how bad it is?"[12] Not every passion, frustration, or injustice is meant to be your God-given calling. That's why it's so important to bring it to God, the One who knit a specific holy discontent within you from the beginning.

> **If you choose to follow your heart wherever it may lead, you will probably walk down paths you were never meant to walk.**

If you choose to follow your heart wherever it may lead, you will probably walk down paths you were never meant to walk. That's why this journey doesn't stop at just discovering your passions; you must also pursue your burning bush experience.

What should you do with what you are driven by? How is God calling someone like you into a partnership with Him to fulfill the specific role you were created for?

I'm still in my early years of ministry, but I've had to (and continue to have to) navigate healthy and unhealthy frustrations in my own journey. One thing I'm incredibly passionate about is church unity. Churches are filled with people – broken, messy, imperfect people. And unfortunately, at times how people choose to act and lead is not a reflection of the love, grace, or hope of Jesus.

I've experienced churches competing with one another rather than coming together to reach the lost. I've seen a few pastors and leaders prioritize their personal agendas, focusing on their image and what influence they have rather than leading congregations with spiritual wisdom and humility.

This issue had the potential to become an unhealthy frustration for me. I began to think maybe ministry wasn't for me. I had to make the conscious choice to give my frustrations to God – to ask Him to help me see through His eyes and to give me wisdom and direction on being part of the solution.

When I did that, God changed my perspective. A driving passion of mine became seeing believers and churches come together to advance the Kingdom.

When I was a young adult pastor in Sacramento, God gave me the desire to launch an event where young adults from the region could come together in one place to worship Him. God made it very clear to me that one person or one church should not drive the event, but a collection of pastors, leaders, and churches should partner together to provide leadership for the event.

By partnering with other young adult pastors in the area, a few hundred people attended the event the first year. But to God's glory (and my amazement), the event has continued to grow into what it is today – a powerful gathering of thousands who worship and pray together. I believe those results are a demonstration of God's favor on a team that was established and continues to operate in unity.

I could have run from a passion God was developing in my heart because I saw no easy solution in sight.

Again, I could have easily let frustration discourage me and drive me away from what God wanted to do. I could have run from a passion God was developing in my heart because I saw no easy solution in sight.

If you find yourself in a similar situation, move toward your frustration as you wait for God to speak to your heart. If and when you see something you just can't stand and you have God's direction, **choose to take action**.

Let me warn you not to force yourself into an unhealthy environment or run toward a situation God has clearly closed the door on. He doesn't expect you to devote yourself to every issue or injustice you care about, nor is He calling you to do that.

Remember to follow the process to determine what *your* holy discontent is – the reason why God created you and has you in this place at this very time. Pay attention to things you are passionate about, but make sure you are continually bringing them to the One who instilled that passion in you.

The process may take some time, but it's never too early or too late to discover what makes you say, "That's all I can stand, and I can't stand any more!"

God is patiently waiting for you to embrace your calling and say yes to helping solve the problem. So, use those passions of yours to drive you in life and shape the ministry He has called you to!

MAKE IT PLAIN

Have you ever thought about the life cycle of a butterfly? Let's quickly review: What starts as an egg hatches into a caterpillar, the caterpillar forms a chrysalis (or what we usually call a cocoon), and finally a butterfly emerges. This typically happens over the course of a few weeks and the cycle begins again.

Now let's think about the differences between a caterpillar and an adult butterfly. It's fascinating how God designed a little bug to transform into a beautiful, winged creature. When you have free time, I encourage you to do some research on your own. (It's worth it, I promise.)

Every stage of the process brings about something the butterfly needs – even the struggle of breaking out of the chrysalis. And it is a struggle, at least in our eyes. But it has to be that way!

Through the difficult process of breaking out—of pushing repeatedly against the inside of the chrysalis—the butterfly develops the strength to fly. If you were to try to "help" the butterfly by cutting open and peeling off the layers, you would actually be hurting it. The butterfly wouldn't be strong enough to fly – and couldn't fulfill the purpose it was created for.

Similarly, the process of identifying your frustrations and learning what you're truly passionate about may feel like a struggle as well. The Bible tells us:

> **When troubles of any kind come your way, consider it an opportunity for great joy. For you know that when your faith is tested, your endurance has a chance to grow. So let it grow, for when your endurance is fully developed, you will be perfect and complete, needing nothing.[13]**

Even though it may be difficult, uncomfortable, and take more time than you thought or hoped, this process

will help you build up your strength, develop patience, establish persistence, and learn to trust. Everything you have been through, are going through, and will go through has a purpose – because God created you and wants someone with your abilities to right some wrongs around you!

Here are three things to consider now as you take advantage of the opportunity to partner with God to ***cover the earth*** with Jesus' love through learning and pursuing your passions.

Be Self-Aware–*Self-awareness* means examining what makes you *you* – your thoughts, emotions, strengths, weaknesses, and beliefs. Sometimes as humans we struggle to assess ourselves objectively. **It's important that we each take time to build self-awareness and understand these traits. It affects our personal growth and development.**

As we've established, our passions are part of who we are. Because God has given each person a holy discontent to change or fix a specific issue in the world, we have to be intentional about learning the *what* and the *why* of our passions, and the *how* of responding

In a letter to the Corinthians, Paul wrote, "Examine yourselves to see if your faith is genuine. Test yourselves."[14]

"Test yourselves" means to evaluate your thoughts, actions, and motives to see if they align with the Word of God. Take time to investigate *what* you are frustrated by and *why* you feel frustrated. Are you upset because you are hanging onto selfish desires, bitterness, and a "holier-than-thou" attitude? Or is it because you see a problem you just can't stand and you sense God inviting you to take part in resolving it?

Many people agree that journaling helps record and process your thoughts, feelings, and energy levels, helping you to become more self-aware. I use a journal that offers several prompts at the end of each day, like, "I was at my best when (blank)," and "I felt unrest when (blank)."

Journaling has helped me to build self-awareness by asking me to stop and reflect on the interactions and events of the day. *If I left a meeting feeling accomplished, why? If I was involved in a conversation that left me feeling angry, why? What left me feeling drained and what gave me energy?* These questions seem simple enough, but they've helped me identify and learn about some of my passions.

God wants you to learn your passions too! **He has called you to a specific role only you can fulfill.** These passions are a gift to help you accomplish that purpose. God says, "I will guide you along the best pathway for your life. I will advise you and watch over you."[15] He promises to lead and guide you in the way you should go. But you still have to take intentional steps to cultivate self-awareness and pursue your holy discontent, seeking His direction throughout the process.

Don't Compare – Someone once said, "Comparison is the thief of joy." Comparison distracts us from what makes us unique – our experiences, skills, strengths, passions – and eats away at our joy and peace. When we're focused on what others have that we don't (or even what we have that they don't), we're not walking in who God has created us to be.

> **Comparison cheapens what He has designed and ignores the plans and purposes He has for us.**

Comparison cheapens what He has designed and ignores the plans and purposes He has for us. That's why Paul directed us to:

> **Pay careful attention to your own work, for then you will get the satisfaction of a job well done, and you won't need to compare yourself to anyone else. For we are each responsible for our own conduct.[17]**

Instead of comparing ourselves to the next person, Paul said we need to examine our own behavior and actions, and assess whether we reflect Jesus or not. It's crucial for you to make personal examination a habit. **Only you are responsible for how you operate within what God has called you to.** Don't start thinking that everyone else is smarter, more talented, more creative, or more – fill in the blank! – than you are.

Just like your giftings, your passions are unique to you. Uniqueness doesn't mean one person is better or more important than another; God intended a variety of passions because of the numerous problems and injustices in our world. And He planned for you to discover your holy discontent in order to ***cover the earth*** with the love of Jesus.

In your ministry journey, you will cross paths with many people who are each passionate about different things. Just as crucial as examining your own work and appreciating your God-given passions, you need to learn to appreciate the passions He has given others. If they correspond with your own passion, focus on working together. If they differ from yours, focus on working together.

As the body of Christ, we are better together! Feeling jealous or envious about others' God-given passions will do nothing but cause insecurity and doubt in your own heart. Alternately, elevating yourself and thinking your passions are closer to God's heart can be hurtful, even detrimental, to your ministry.

The Bible says we are clay and God is the potter, and "we are all formed by [his] hand."[18] **The passion and holy discontent you possess is no mistake—it is an intentional gift from God. Getting stuck in the trap of comparison will only hinder your ability to fulfill the specific work He has called you to.**

Guard Your Heart – You can't always trust your heart. What you fill it with influences your desires, motivations, and even your morals. And what is truly in your heart will be revealed through your thoughts, words, and actions. That's why Scripture tells us, "Guard your heart above all else, for it determines the course of your life."[19]

Guarding your heart is a twofold approach: First, fill your heart with biblical truth. Spend time in God's presence, praying and reading the Bible. Then identify how He is calling you to resolve the issues you are passionate about. The second part of guarding your heart is actually guarding that biblical truth. If we're not careful, it's easy to forget or ignore what God says and live our lives based on what we think or how we feel about what's going on around us.

Earlier, we talked about how frustration can easily turn into bitterness, anger, resentment, or pride if we're not surrendering it to God and allowing *Him* to use our frustration to fuel us into action. We need to depend on God daily, asking the One who created us the same thing David asked: "Search me, O God, and know my heart; test me and know my anxious thoughts. Point out anything in me that offends you, and lead me along the path of everlasting life."[20]

David knew firsthand the only way to trust his heart—and everything in it—was to give it to God. We would do well to follow David's example. This posture of humility is critical when asking God how He wants us to resolve our holy discontent.

But this surrender is not about challenging God to search your heart and find what's wrong – quite the opposite, actually. If we follow our heart without checking it, we may end up in places we were never called to, doing things God never asked us to do.

So, asking God to search and test you is not arrogant; doing so protects you. He knows what you can't stand

and why you can't stand it. **He knows what you should do with your holy discontent. He knows the process you will undergo to fulfill the role you were created for.**

But you will need to intentionally guard the truth and passions within your heart against any negative, selfish feelings that threaten to take root. This is how you can live out your holy discontent, partnering with God to redeem and restore this world.

Take some time to answer the following questions and share them with someone you trust.

1. From this chapter, what stuck out to you the most and why?

2. What are some frustrations you currently have in your life? Do these frustrations match the issues you feel passionate about?

3. What steps can you start taking today to develop self-awareness?

4. What practical things can you do to guard your heart?

Check out more resources regarding learning passions at:

called.ag.org

Notes

1 *Merriam-Webster*, s.v. "discontent (n.)" accessed February 17, 2021, https://www.merriam-webster.com/dictionary/discontent.

2 Fandom, Popeye the Sailorpedia, "List of Catchphrases," accessed February 17, 2021, https://popeye.fandom.com/wiki/List_of_catchphrases.

3 Exodus 1:12.

4 Exodus 1:22.

5 Exodus 2:5–6.

6 Exodus 2:11.

7 Exodus 2:12.

8 Exodus 3:2–10.

9 Biography.com Editors, "Rosa Parks Biography," *The Biography.com Website*, A&E Television Networks, April 2, 2014, accessed February 14, 2021, https://www.biography.com/activist/rosa-parks.

10 Beth Grant, *Courageous Compassion: Confronting Social Injustice God's Way* (Springfield, MO: Gospel Publishing House, 2014), 15.

11 Hal Donaldson, *Disruptive Compassion: Becoming the Revolutionary You Were Born to Be* (Grand Rapids, MI: Zondervan, 2019), 32.

12 Jeremiah 17:9.

13 James 1:2–4.

14 2 Corinthians 13:5.

15 Psalm 32:8.

16 Galatians 6:4–5.

17 Isaiah 64:8.

18 Proverbs 4:23.

19 Psalm 139:23–24.

CHAPTER SIX
NEVER ARRIVE

The Walt Disney Company, one of the biggest media and entertainment companies in the world, topped *Forbes* magazine's "World's Best Regarded Companies" list in 2018. Disney scored high when it came to things like "trustworthiness, social conduct, [and] performance."[1]

But what *really* makes Disney the best?

Walt Disney

Walt Disney said it this way: **"Disneyland will never be completed, as long as there is imagination left in the world."[2]** Simply put, the company never arrives!

A company like Disney could easily adopt the mentality that they have arrived. They could coast straight into complacency with their billions of dollars, never imagining or engineering anything new. But employees live by Walt's statement in everything they do – amusement parks, digital entertainment, products and more – because of the possibility of what *could* be. **They resist complacency in**

yesterday's successes and continue to choose growth, moving forward purposefully. But how does Mickey Mouse relate to your situation?

Setting goals can motivate us to work hard and stay focused. But, society often leads us to believe that – whatever they are – reaching our goals is the final destination. *Graduate from high school. Get married. Land a dream job. Go on a missions trip. Grow a youth ministry. Become a lead pastor.* While all these goals are commendable, don't fool yourself into thinking that once you have achieved your goal, that's it, you're done! You have arrived and have nothing else to do, so you can settle in.

Wrong. You should always ask the question, "What's next?"

Now, I'm not saying you should gloss over an achievement without celebrating or at least acknowledging what you accomplished. Many people say that what you celebrate or recognize, you will repeat.

But growth—specifically *healthy* growth—doesn't happen when you are content with an outcome. That's what I mean by "arriving." Here are some things that happen when we think we've arrived:

- We dismiss the value of the process.
- We focus on the result.
- We no longer allow for growth.

These concepts remain true regardless of whether it's a person, an organization, or a ministry with these thoughts.

Healthy growth only happens if and when you have the mindset that you will "never arrive."

Benjamin Franklin once said, "When you are finished changing, you're finished."[3] With his long list of accomplishments – as one of our nation's founding fathers, politician, inventor, scientist, and author, to name a few – he spoke from experience, rejecting complacency in favor of change and personal growth.

Benjamin Franklin

Think about that for a moment. *If you're not changing, you're done.*

As a leader, and especially as a ministry leader, that thought should alarm you. You should always have areas of life in which you can grow. (If you can't think of any, you're not thinking hard enough!) Make a conscious decision to embrace change and commit to healthy growth so you can be a part of ***covering the earth*** with the love of Jesus.

Begin reflecting now: *What are some dreams and goals I have? Are these goals things I want to do, or think I should do? Do these goals align with my gifts and passions? Will this help or hurt my called journey?*

These reflection questions are just examples of what you need to ask yourself throughout life. **Remember, if you think**

that you have arrived, then your focus is too narrow. If you only look at the outcome, you discount the value of the entire process. And God values the process.

Jesus said, "I am the true grapevine, and my Father is the gardener. He cuts off every branch of mine that doesn't produce fruit, and he prunes the branches that do bear fruit so they will produce even more."[4] This metaphor of pruning speaks of an ongoing process, cutting away dead leaves and branches to allow for and promote new growth.

In real life, if gardeners want fruit, they don't have the luxury of sitting back and letting the trees grow willy-nilly. Even if the previous season saw incredible growth and healthy fruit, gardeners take time to assess the new growth, trim away what is unwanted or harmful, and allow room for the new branches to accomplish their purpose.

Celebrate the fruit of your labor, whatever that may look like, but remember, a season of success does not permit a lifetime of complacency.

A level of expectation shows up in this verse in John 15 – we expect growth, but it's a continuous process to strive to "never arrive." Celebrate the fruit of your labor, whatever that may look like, but remember, a season of success does not permit a lifetime of complacency.

Humility is a key characteristic of someone who has a "never arrive" approach. A humble person is not proud or arrogant; a humble *believer* also has the understanding that they are where they are and have what they have because of God. Scripture tells us, "The LORD detests the proud; they will surely be punished."[5] *Detests* is a strong word, but it was used intentionally. God hates, loathes, despises, and rejects the proud.

No room for conceit, overconfidence, or superiority exists in the life of a believer because those characteristics are not from God. It's a sinful mindset that will lead to your ruin.[6] Those words may sound harsh, but they are true. Remember that in chapter 2 we talked about how the devil was cast out of heaven when pride filled his heart? The consequences of pride, or having a prideful "arrival" outlook, eliminate the possibility of healthy growth.

A few years ago, I was invited to speak at an event. The organizers had heard me preach a message once before and they requested that I share that specific message at their event. As a communicator, I know when I strike out and when I knock something out of the park, and I knew that message had been a grand slam! So, in preparation for this event, I did the opposite – I didn't prepare.

The first time I preached this message I had done exceptionally well, so why would round two be any different? I didn't review my notes, I didn't restudy any of the Scriptures, I didn't go over any part of my message. And you know what happened? **I walked into that event pridefully thinking, I've got this, when I actually didn't have it.** That preaching experience was one of the worst I've ever had because I thought I had already arrived. I was overconfident and dismissed any thought of depending on God during this message as I had depended on Him the first time I preached it. Not depending on God is dangerous, so let my mistake be a warning to others to purposely avoid the "arrival" frame of mind.

Humble yourself and acknowledge that God has brought you to where you are. Doing this creates a dependency on Him and creates space to continue discovering your gifts, learning your passions, and becoming who He created you to be.

Humble yourself and acknowledge that God has brought you to where you are.

Sometimes we view a humble person as meek, unassertive, overmodest, or submissive – but that's not always the case. Pastor and author Rick Warren said, **"This is true humility: not thinking less of ourselves but thinking of ourselves less."**[7] It's possible to be confident and humble at the same time – confident in your identity and God-given abilities, but humble enough to ask questions and learn from others.

Be aware of something called false humility because, as one writer warns, it is "pridefulness in disguise. . . . . Examples of false humility include deflecting praise we truly deserve, fishing for compliments to draw attention to ourselves, 'humble-bragging' (talking about how humble we are), falsely portraying helplessness or a lack of power, and self-deprecating humor."[8]

Seeing humility as a weakness can play into the "arrival" mindset and inhibit your growth, just as practicing false humility. Nothing is wrong with admitting you don't know it all (who does?), seeking out people who are smarter and wiser than you are, and being open to any knowledge they have to share. That's what confident, humble people do anyway. On the other hand, the insecure ones who think they have arrived and know everything won't ask questions.

In writing this chapter, I reached out to a man I have looked up to in life and ministry for years – Pastor Robert Douglas. For someone who has experienced as much success in his ministry career as he has, Pastor Robert somehow continues to remain humble and teachable at seventy years old. He is the epitome of "never arriving."

I wanted to try to understand how he does it. When I called him, I just opened with what I saw in him: a leader who, although successful, operates out of a willingness to learn and pursues healthy growth. His response? **"If that is true, all the glory goes to God . . . I do not take pride in my abilities, but I have full confidence in what God can do through me."[9]**

Pastor Robert Douglas

I mean, come on! A person doesn't get more humble than that, especially when they believe it and say it in all sincerity. People like Pastor Robert know they are a work in progress, and with every accomplishment and success, God is bringing them one step closer to fulfilling their purpose on earth. **They reject complacency and embrace change and growth, continuing to set new goals and see things that could be.**

Throughout our conversation, Pastor Robert revealed a couple of foundational blocks he focuses on in his life. The first is learning the art of listening. He told me, "When you take time to listen to others, you can learn from others. They will teach you and you will teach them, regardless of their age."

The problem is that most of us don't truly listen. Typically the way we communicate is to listen so we can reply, waiting patiently (or impatiently) until it's our turn to talk. That's not true listening because instead of paying attention to what the other person is telling us, we are already thinking about what we are going to say.

Intentionally or not, a selfish, prideful attitude blocks us from learning from others and hinders our growth. **That's why it's so important to learn and practice listening to understand, instead of listening to respond.** That means putting your phone away, using eye contact, not interrupting, asking questions when appropriate, and only offering your opinion or advice when asked. Actively listening to – and hearing – what others say adds value to your life and assists your growth.

Pastor Robert also stressed the importance of being grateful as a second foundational block. He specifically talked about how blessed he was to have air conditioning in his home and car, a bed to sleep in, and being married to an amazing wife.

Practicing gratitude has a multitude of benefits.

We commonly take things like comfort and relationships for granted, but that's not an excuse. Practicing gratitude has a multitude of benefits. Research shows that, "Grateful people tend to be healthy and happy. They exhibit lower levels of stress and depression, cope better with adversity and sleep better. They tend to be happier and more satisfied with life."[10]

That's why Pastor Robert has made a habit of reminding himself of the good things in life, as well as knowing from whom those good things come.[11] **As believers, daily expressing thanks is an appropriate response to the grace, generosity, kindness, and faithfulness of God.** Purposely practicing gratitude guards against the "arrival" state of mind.

Truthfully, without God we can't do anything. It's important to remember that we are part of the big picture, but not the big picture itself. We would be crazy to think that we could perfect, let alone finish, what God has started.[12]

And people like Pastor Robert who have experienced ministry success time and again know and live by that knowledge. Let's circle back to the pruning metaphor discussed earlier in this chapter. Jesus said, "I am the vine; you are the branches. Those who remain in me, and I in them, will produce much fruit. For apart from me you can do nothing."[13]

Something else will always exist to give you reason to reject and move past "arrival"—a new goal, dream, or hope. We have to rely on God and trust the process in order to experience healthy growth and continuous fruitfulness. What He wants to do in and through us will be far more fulfilling and rewarding than what we could do on our own. And that knowledge will help keep us from ever thinking we have arrived.

MAKE IT PLAIN

I've intentionally included the word *healthy* before *growth* in this chapter. The truth is, we are all growing! **Growth is an ongoing process; if something isn't growing, it's dying.** But, growth doesn't automatically mean health; bad things like rumors, weeds, and cancer grow too.

So, it's not whether you are going to grow or not, but whether you are going to pursue health, humility, purpose, and ultimately God's calling on your life. It's up to you to decide, but I challenge you to consider doing these four things regularly to resist the "arrival" mindset and posture yourself for healthy growth!

Ask Questions—You will find immense value in asking questions and seeking out information. If you are not asking questions, you are not learning; if you are not learning, you are not growing. You've no doubt heard this old saying: "Curiosity killed the cat." It is a warning to overly curious people that asking may get them into trouble. But I don't like that. Curiosity can be good. Albert Einstein once said, "The important thing is not to stop questioning. Curiosity has its own reason for existence."[14]

"The important thing is not to stop questioning. Curiosity has its own reason for existence."

Healthy curiosity is incredibly beneficial to your personal growth. Even if you think your question is dumb, obvious, or ill-informed, you can still find value in asking it. Asking questions shows your willingness to learn and outweighs fear, complacency, or pride.

Asking questions and looking for answers is also biblical. Jesus was clear when He told His disciples:

> **"Keep on asking, and you will receive what you ask for. Keep on seeking, and you will find. Keep on knocking, and the door will be opened to you. For everyone who asks, receives. Everyone who seeks, finds. And to everyone who knocks, the door will be opened."[15]**

Asking, seeking, and knocking require necessary action on our part if we are to grow in knowledge and wisdom. God wants us to ask! Speaking to the prophet Jeremiah, God said, "Ask me and I will tell you remarkable secrets you do not know about things to come."[16] The cool thing is we can take hold of that promise too – asking questions opens the door to know God better and experience His Word.

Learn from Anyone – Graduation is a way we measure success. From kindergarten to high school and college graduations, even "graduating" from internships and entry-level positions, these important steps are everywhere in our culture. They're not a bad thing; graduation is often a long-term goal we can focus on and strive to meet. **We can also identify areas of growth or improvement as we work toward graduation.**

However, issues arise when we apply this graduation mindset to our standard of learning. Here's what I mean: It's easy to think that once you graduate from middle school, you can't learn anything from a middle schooler. You may think a middle schooler can only learn from you because you are older, smarter, and wiser, while they are still at a level you've already graduated from.

At some point in your life, you won't have anywhere to graduate from; you'll have earned a doctoral degree, reached the highest-paying job, or gained expertise in your field. You will be able to say, "Been there, done that," to everyone around you because they are still in situations or seasons you were previously in.

You may think, *Who can teach me now?* That is the very definition of an "arrival" way of thinking! We've established that when we stop valuing the process and no longer prioritize learning, we stop growing – a very unhealthy and dangerous place.

The Bible tells us that God can use anyone (or anything) to accomplish His purposes in the world. That means He can use anyone He wants to teach us! We do have to make the choice to humble ourselves and remain open to learning from others to avoid missing out on what the Holy Spirit wants to do in our own heart, mind, and soul.

He can use anyone He wants to teach us!

We must pay attention because He will often use the unlikeliest people. Think about Moses freeing the Israelites, Paul (a former Pharisee) preaching the gospel, and Balaam's donkey speaking to him.

Wait, what? You can read the whole story in Numbers 22, but long story short, God made a donkey talk to get the attention of someone who was being disobedient. It seems strange, maybe even a little excessive, but it was a crucial teaching moment for Balaam. God shows love and care for His people when He uses whatever means necessary to teach us something.

If God can use a donkey to teach a man, who am I to say that I can't learn from someone simply because I've "graduated" from a previous position? Be open to listening and learning from anyone at any time.

Don't Believe the Hype – Flattery is your enemy. Defined as "insincere or excessive praise," flattery can be a form of manipulation and often plays into a person's pride and arrogance.[17] Everyone likes to receive compliments and hear good things about themselves, but at times people will praise and honor you simply to gain or control something. That's not genuine praise and it can be dangerous.

If we're only focused on being successful and showing everyone how great we are, when we receive praise, it could ruin us. Our attitude toward flattery will foster an "arrival" mindset, stunt our growth, turn our focus inward, and belittle what God has done and is doing in us. This is where confident humility comes in. We can be confident in who we are and our God-given abilities, but we also know we can't do anything eternally significant without God.

In the Book of Acts, we read about the Roman officer Cornelius who had a vision of an angel telling him to send for Peter. When Peter arrived, "Cornelius fell at his feet and worshiped him. But Peter pulled him up and said, 'Stand up! I'm a human being just like you!' "[18]

Although genuine, Cornelius mistakenly worshipped Peter who quickly refused it. As easy as it would have been for Peter to accept the praise, he knew the success he experienced was a result of God working through him. He didn't let the praise of people influence or determine his mindset in life.

He didn't let the praise of people influence or determine his mindset in life.

Here's a different example. I love the scene in the movie, *The Dark Knight Rises*, where Batman and the antagonist, Bane, meet for the first time. This meeting took place when organized crime was at an all-time low and the city of Gotham was experiencing peace. Because of this, Batman retired; he lost the motivation to continue training and stay active, so he became out of shape. In their first encounter Bane had no trouble beating Batman. In the midst of their fight, Bane said, **"Peace has cost you your strength. Victory has defeated you."**[19]

On the surface, it felt like Batman had arrived, but in reality, it was a false sense of "arrival." His season of victory resulted in complacency, and in that moment, his complacency defeated him. He believed the hype about what peace would do for the city, but peace did nothing for him.

Let me say it again: **Don't believe the hype. A season of success doesn't permit a lifetime of complacency.**

Seek Different Voices – This may seem similar to "Learn from Anyone," but there's an active intentionality behind it. We tend to like and gravitate toward people who are like us – it's safe, it's comfortable, it's peaceful, you get to be right most of the time – and that's not always a bad thing. But only hanging out with people who are the same as we are can be dangerous. How can we expect to learn and grow if we're only surrounded by people with similar backgrounds, attitudes, opinions, interests, and values? We can't.

If we continue hanging out with people like us, possibly no one will challenge our thinking or offer new ways of doing something. We will probably not consider new ideas or perspectives or be exposed to cultures different from our own. Our bad attitudes or negative viewpoints will possibly not be rejected or corrected. **Comfort is the beginning of complacency; our comfort zones will not allow for healthy growth.** It's crucial in your life and ministry to consistently go out of your way to find people who different from you so you can combat this false feeling of "arrival."

The Bible is clear about the purpose in our differences. We are *all* created in God's image, but each aspect of who we are – looks, backgrounds, gifts, passions – reflects Him in a unique way and equips us for the calling on our lives.[20] So, prioritize seeking out different voices, building and investing in relationships with those who look, think, and act differently than you. Great leaders embrace healthy growth.

We complement each other in God's design for this world and work best when we work together to ***cover the earth*** with the love of Jesus. The variety in our differences forms the perfect body of Christ, which is how God intended it from the beginning!

Take some time to answer the following questions and share them with someone you trust.

1. From this chapter, what stuck out to you the most and why?

2. What is one area you would like to experience growth in?

3. How can you remain humble when God is giving you success?

4. What are some things you can do to make sure you never arrive?

Check out more resources regarding never arriving at:

called.ag.org

Notes

1 Andrea Murphy, "Global 2000: The World's Best Regarded Companies 2018." *Forbes* magazine, September 12, 2018, accessed February 17, 2021, www.forbes.com/sites/andreamurphy/2018/09/12/global-2000-the-worlds-best-regarded-companies-2018/?sh=970fcfa7e7b2.

2 Walt Disney as quoted by Sharon Slater, "'Disney land Forever' Fireworks Spectacular Announced," *Disneyland Resort* (blog) January 28, 2015, https:disneyparks.disney.go.com/blog/autnor/shawn-slater/.

3 Benjamin Franklin, *GoodReads Quotes*, accessed February 17, 2021, https://www.goodreads.com/quotes/18415-when-You-are-finished-changing-you-refinished#:~:text=Quote%20by%20Benjamin%20Franklin%3A%20%E2%80%9CWhen,%2C%20you're%20finished.%E2%80%9D.

4 John 15:1–2.

5 Proverbs 16:5.

6 Proverbs 16:18.

7 Rick Warren, *The Purpose Driven Life: What on Earth Am I Here For?* (Grand Rapids, MI: Zondervan, 2002), 265.

8 Randy Conley, "4 Ways to Overcome the Danger of False Humility," *Leading with Trust*, October 6, 2019, accessed February 17, 2021, https://leadingwithtrust.com/2019/10/06/4-ways-to-overcome-the-danger-of-false-humility/.

9 Robert Douglas, interview with the author, August 27, 2020.

10 Richard Gunderman and The Conversation, "Why being thankful is so good for your health," *CNN, Cable News Network*, November 28, 2019, accessed February 17, 2021, https://www.cnn.com/2019/11/28/health/thanksgiving-gratitude-conversation-wellness/index.html.

11 James 1:17.

12 Galatians 3:3.

13 John 15:5.

14 William Miller, "Old Man's Advice to Youth: 'Never Lose a Holy Curiosity,' " *Life*, May 2, 1955, 64.

15 Matthew 7:7–8.
16 Jeremiah 33:3.
17 *Merriam-Webster*, s.v. "flattery (n.)," accessed February 17, 2021, https://www.merriam-webster.com/dictionary/flattery.
18 Acts 10:3–5, 25–26.
19 *The Dark Knight Rises*, directed by Christopher Nolan (2012; Burbank, CA: Warner Brothers Pictures).
20 Genesis 1:27.

EPILOGUE

Called. It's so much more than just a word (or a book title). It's a mandate given to each one of us by the Creator of the world to go and ***cover the earth*** with the love of Jesus.[1] You may already know what role you're called to – pastor, missionary, evangelist, church planter, or the like – or you may still be seeking God's direction. The important thing to understand is that it is *your* calling.

I hope you now know and believe God fearfully and wonderfully created you because He wanted *you* to fulfill a specific part of His plan, and He planned what He wanted you to do a long time ago.[2] No matter your age, background, talents, triumphs, mistakes, doubts, you have been called on purpose for a unique purpose.

Now that you are done reading this book, does this mean you are totally done? No way! This is just the beginning of your journey. The goal of this book is to give you a road map for healthy ministry. **But for a road map to be beneficial, there needs to be a road—a foundation—you can successfully drive on.** These six principles have to be built on a healthy foundation for them to last in your life and in your ministry.

The only way that can happen is if you truly know Jesus and have a personal relationship with Him. You might be thinking, *Of course I know Jesus! That's how I was called to ministry in the first place. That's why I'm reading this book.* Consider this: **What Jesus do you know?** The answer to this question will determine the strength of the foundation you build your life and ministry on.

Perception is a powerful thing; the way we view, understand, or believe things to be dictates our lens on reality. No two people will ever perceive things the same way since they won't have the same life experiences. That is why it's important to acknowledge while perception can become our reality, it's not everyone's reality. What's more, if our perception is influenced by lies or misinformation, it can negatively affect our perspective since we filter everything through that lens.

Here's just one example: The Bible says numerous times that God is our Father.[3] Based on your relationship with your earthly father and how you view him, this could either be a positive description or a horrible one. If our perception of our earthly father is good, then these verses might bring feelings of comfort and love. The opposite is also true if our perspective of our earthly father is bad – feelings of frustration or hurt may surface. It's likely your idea of God will follow that as well! It's all based on our lens. **So, even though you feel like you know Jesus, your version of Him may be skewed based on the lens you have formed through your personal experiences.**

Unfortunately for many people, they have a flawed picture of Jesus because they've allowed human nature to inform their idea of who He is. If your relationship with Jesus feels heavy – a burden weighing you down, a pressure to perform, shame or guilt for what you've done – then your perspective is off.

Jesus said,

> **"Come to me, all of you who are weary and carry heavy burdens, and I will give you rest. Take my yoke upon you. Let me teach you, because I am humble and gentle at heart, and you will find rest for your souls. For my yoke is easy to bear, and the burden I give you is light."[4]**

A relationship with God is not a chore or something you have to do to be a "good Christian." There should be an excitement to spend intimate time with the One who created you, who loves you the most, who desires to have a personal relationship with *you*.

Not only do we need to make sure that our understanding of Jesus is biblical, but our personal identity must also be formed by what Scripture says. In what do you currently find your identity? Is it your school achievements? Your appearance? Your athleticism? Your artistic ability? Your relationships? **Since permanency is not promised to us in any of these areas, the foundation of our identity is shaky at best—who we believe we are can change as the things around us change.**

But the Bible offers us a firm foundation. Thankfully it relies on something – or rather, *Someone* – outside ourselves. Simply put, identity is about who God says we are. In Ephesians 1, Paul wrote an incredible description of us when we come to faith in Jesus: we are blessed with spiritual blessing, unconditionally loved, chosen, adopted, forgiven, and united with Christ.[5]

Identity is about who God says we are.

Notice how none of those things relies on anything we could do in our own power, but they are freely given to us because Jesus took our place and died on the cross for our sins.[6] Now that you are a child of God[7] and "your real life is hidden with Christ,"[8] that takes a lot of pressure off to try to earn what we already possess. **Basing your identity on whose you are instead of who the world says you are means your identity won't change based on external circumstances.** This gives you the strength and confidence to share His love with those around you.

These are reasons why perspective is such a big deal. Skewed perspectives can cause people to spend their whole life without discovering the truth and freedom that comes from Christ. As people called into ministry, we have the opportunity to help others walk in that freedom, which is why we must make sure our foundation is healthy.

So, take some time to inspect your heart and really reflect: Do I understand my true identity? Do I have a

Bible-informed awareness of who God is? Is my perspective based on Scripture, or on a broken, imperfect world? Some of these things won't change or be "fixed" overnight – it will be an ongoing, but necessary, process and that's okay! Remember, God values the process. Resist the temptation to rush into any aspect of your ministry journey, and allow Him to teach you, develop you, equip you, and guide you so you can be effective in ***covering the earth*** with the love of Jesus.

Remember, God values the process.

As you begin walking this journey, embrace the call God has on your life. We are all called to share the gospel, but spending time in prayer is a must to determine if God is calling you to a vocation in the church. Ministry isn't for the apathetic or passive, and it isn't for those who are pursuing fame or glory. James wrote, "Dear brothers and sisters, not many of you should become teachers in the church, for we who teach will be judged more strictly."[9] This isn't to discourage you or scare you into running from your call, but being a ministry leader is a huge responsibility and should not be taken lightly. **You have to pursue the plan God has for you, not anyone else, and spending time in prayer is the best place to start.**

You also should be seeking the Holy Spirit – the Advocate, Helper, and Comforter God gives us.[10] Paul wrote, "[God] washed away our sins, giving us a new birth and new life through the Holy Spirit," meaning empowerment by the

Holy Spirit starts when we come to faith in God.[11] After salvation comes the baptism in the Holy Spirit. In Acts, after Jesus was crucified and resurrected, He appeared to the disciples and commanded them to stay in Jerusalem until God sent the Holy Spirit as promised. Jesus knew they would need to experience the baptism in the Spirit to effectively share the gospel message.[12]

You have access to the same Spirit as the disciples, and you need the Spirit's help just as much as they did. Seek Him out! Ask Him to do a work *in* you, making you look more like Jesus. Ask Him to work *through* you and your words, gifts, and passions. And ask to work *with* Him to accomplish God's will. Don't try to walk this ministry journey without Him.

Finally, plan ahead. While seeking God's will for your life through prayer and reading His Word is necessary in the life of a believer, there comes a point when you need to make plans and move forward. As you think about what college you want to attend, what internships to apply for, or researching where you want to work, you can't just sit around waiting for God to make everything come together, blaming Him when it doesn't happen.

You were given free will to make decisions and choose things for yourself; however, pursuing a ministry call requires that you use wisdom in the choices you consider. Make sure that everything you plan for is out of your love for God and a desire to fulfill the purpose He has for you. The writer of Proverbs said, "We can make our plans, but the LORD determines our steps."[13]

As you seek God and plan ahead, hold every plan you make with an open hand. You don't have the luxury of seeing into the future, but God does. It's wise to make your plans but then release them to the One who knows the beginning from the end. If you do that and trust Him, He will direct you in the way that is best for you.

You don't have the luxury of seeing into the future, but God does.

You are a part of God's plan to ***cover the earth*** with the gospel. I hope this book has helped confirm the specific call He has on your life as well as given you practical steps to begin pursuing that call.

Now, as you get ready for the journey, know that I pray you grow in your knowledge and understanding of who God is and who He says you are. I pray you find joy and peace and fulfillment in living your ministry calling. I pray you find the strength to establish habits and disciplines that will last you a lifetime. I pray you cultivate a heart to serve people in your home, church, and community. I pray you are surrounded with people who will develop, encourage, and stretch you. I pray you walk confidently in your gifts and use them as tools to share the gospel message. I pray your passions and what you can't stand drive you in life and ministry. I pray you never arrive, instead choosing to continue learning and pursuing healthy growth.

Above all I pray this: " 'May the LORD bless you and protect you. May the LORD smile on you and be gracious to you. May the LORD show you his favor and give you his peace.' "[14]

Amen.

Notes

1 Matthew 28:18–20.
2 Ephesians 2:10.
3 Psalm 68:5; Isaiah 64:8; Matthew 23:9; Romans 8:15; 2 Corinthians 6:18; 1 John 3:1.
4 Matthew 11:28–30.
5 Ephesians 1:3–14.
6 John 3:16; Romans 5:8; 1 Peter 3:18.
7 John 1:12.
8 Colossians 3:3.
9 James 3:1.
10 John 14:16.
11 Titus 3:5.
12 Acts 1:4, 8.
13 Proverbs 16:9.
14 Numbers 6:24–26.